A LOVE *Beyond* LIFE

MY JOURNEY THROUGH GRIEF TO EVERLASTING CONNECTION

BRENDA L. FLETCHER

Build. Buzz. Launch. Media & Publishing
8718 Redondo Drive
Dallas, TX 75218
BuildBuzzLaunch.com

Book cover and interior design by Monkey C Media

First Edition
Printed in the United States of America

ISBN: 978-1-7352966-2-3 (trade paperback)
ISBN: 978-1-7352966-3-0 (ebook)

Library of Congress Control Number: 2021943267

IN MEMORY OF
TODD FLETCHER

You're in our hearts
In the sounds and actions of our children and grandchildren
You're in the flight of a red-tailed hawk
You're the sweet whisper in my ear
You're in the trees, in the air
You are everywhere!

Love you forever, xoxoxo

DEDICATION

Todd and I dedicate this book to our daughter Alexia, son Dakota, and grandson Jackson. Todd felt such enormous joy from his family. I thought long about the multitude of pictures I could have put in this book, so many beautiful pictures of family and friends. But, I think these two pictures sum it all up nicely. There is life, love and death, and the one thing that is constant within all of this is love. We are all beautifully connected with love.

This is a picture of the first time Todd held his grandson. Jackson was a few weeks shy of his second birthday when Todd passed. Todd and Jackson shared a close connection. This second picture is from a day we spent together as a family where Jackson helped grandpa do yard work. Both incredibly beautiful days.

Alexia hung pictures of Todd above Jackson's crib shortly after he passed. Just about every morning, Alexia would find the picture of Todd holding him for the first time clutched in Jackson's tiny fingers. She would take a moment to unfold his fingers and tape it back up above his crib.

As I write this, Jackson is about to have his 10th birthday, and he still remains bonded to his grandpa through this love beyond life.

Thank you to our lovely children, Alexia and Dakota, and thank you to all of our wonderful family and friends for all your love and support always.

CONTENTS

INTRODUCTION

This is a love story. A story about how love never dies. For thirty years my husband Todd and I shared an amazing life together. When Todd was suddenly killed in a motorcycle accident, I immediately started searching for ways to keep him with me. I bought lots of books about connecting with people on the other side. I kept them on the bed, in the spot where Todd slept.

Since his death, I've discovered new ways to be with my husband. Our love has continued to grow and deepen while I am physically here on earth and he is in heaven; we've found ways to meet each other in the middle. This book contains the lessons I've learned from loss and the joy that awaits us on the other side of grief when we discover that love lasts forever.

I suspect for most people who experience the death of a loved one, the same is universally true; we just want them back. And since we can't have them physically back, we want the next best thing —to communicate with them again. We don't want to lose their presence in our lives.

My hope is that people suffering from loss and those who are supporting them will gain better insight and understanding of the grief process from reading our story. Feelings of separation cause great suffering, but loved ones on the other side are always trying to connect with us. Anyone can learn to tune into them.

Todd is still very much present in my life, with me every day, guiding me in beautiful and magical ways. Through the signs he gives me and the connection we continue to share, I know his love for me will never die. It may sound like a miracle, and in many ways it is, but communicating with our loved ones who have passed is readily available to all. There are many ways to connect. Todd and I will show you how.

1

SHATTERED

I started my day on Wednesday, July 24, 2013, feeling rushed. I'd decided last-minute to pick some flowers for my co-worker Joy, which made my tight schedule even tighter. Joy is obsessed with British royalty. The day before, I'd teased her over lunch at our favorite Japanese restaurant when Prince William and Kate were about to present their new son George to the public on television.

"Look, there he is!" I'd said repeatedly.

Eager to see the newest member of the royal family, she'd taken the bait and turned to look over at the television every single time.

It had been funny then, but the next morning I was feeling a bit guilty. So, I plucked some daisies and irises from the garden, jammed them into a red coffee cup, and ran off to work. On my way out, I hollered, "I love you, see you later, babe!" to my husband Todd, who was still in bed.

I delivered the flowers to Joy, but by the time I made it to my office, I wasn't feeling well. Unable to shake my uneasiness, around 9:30 a.m. I emailed my boss and took a sick day.

Things just didn't feel right as I drove back home. I couldn't wait to settle back in at home with my two dogs and wait for Todd to return. I was confident being home with Todd would make me feel better. I could always rely on that. My husband worked the evening shift in production at Crown Cork and Seal, an aerosol can factory. He was running a couple of errands that morning but would stop home for an hour or two before going into work.

He'd eat lunch, and then I would get to spend a little time with him before he showered, put on the work pants he left draped over the bottom of the bed frame, and prepared the dinner he took in a lunchbox to eat during his shift. He'd kiss and hug me goodbye before getting on his Harley Davidson, a bike he loved almost as much as he loved me, our two kids, and our two-year-old grandson.

I had just gotten home and changed out of my work clothes when the doorbell rang. I knew it wasn't someone familiar because our friends and family used the side entrance. Our dogs, Ruby and Stanley, barked so loudly that I put them in the basement before I answered the door.

When I finally pulled the door open, a sheriff's officer stood on the top step, large brown hat in one hand. Behind him was a middle-aged woman in a yellow vest, the kind a road worker usually wears, with reflectors on it. A tag on the front read, "Chaplain."

"Hello ma'am, is this the residence of Todd Fletcher?" the officer asked.

"Yes," I answered slowly. The only time the police had come to our door before was when Todd's horses had gotten loose from the pasture. Something about the officer's subdued demeanor told me that he'd come for more than a broken fence.

"Is this the home of Todd Fletcher, ma'am?" the officer repeated. "Are you his wife?"

I nodded. My stomach clenched at the urgency in the officer's voice. The look on his face said he wished he was anywhere else but there.

"May we come in?"

My heart sank as I reluctantly moved aside and pulled the door open wider.

"Mrs. Fletcher, is anyone else here with you?" The officer's voice softened as he stepped into the house. Suddenly my knees felt like they were going to give out on me. I took a few steps back until I was in the dining room. I gripped a chair back to steady myself.

"Mrs. Fletcher, I'm sorry to tell you that your husband has been in an accident." The officer looked down at the hat in his hands, then back up into my eyes. "Please, ma'am," he was insistent, "Is there someone here with you or someone we can call?"

When I didn't answer, he repeated somberly, "Ma'am, your husband was in an accident. I'm very sorry to tell you he died at the scene."

Disbelief flooded me. I stood frozen, unable to take in the officer's words. *It couldn't be true. Todd couldn't be dead. He was just out running errands.*

"My son Dakota is downstairs in the basement." I heard the words fly out of my mouth before I could think about how awful it would be for my eighteen-year-old to learn that his father was dead.

Before I could stop him, the officer stepped through the dining room and down the basement steps. The chaplain moved nearer to me.

"Who can we call for you?" She placed her hand gently on my shoulder. "I'm so sorry for your loss." She was a soft-spoken middle-aged woman with a kind face. I could tell from her demeanor that she had done this many times before.

A million thoughts raced through my mind. *This lady is just doing her job. She's trying to keep me calm and figure out who she can call to come be with me in the best way she can. This is just another day at work for her, while this is the very worst day of my life.*

I'll never forget the shock and despair on my son's face when he came up the basement steps with the sheriff. The officer guided us into the living room and had us sit down. Dakota and I clung to each other on the couch while the sheriff explained that a semi-truck had struck Todd's motorcycle, sending him flying several feet in the air. Todd had been wearing his helmet but was killed on impact.

The room was spinning. I didn't want to hear any more, but at the same time, I needed to know what had happened. Images of my husband being thrown in the air and crashing onto the hard ground played out in my mind like a bad movie. Only it wasn't a movie. It was real.

Or was it?

I shifted back and forth from taking in the information to thoughts of denial. I imagined the sheriff saying, "Mrs. Fletcher, we made a terrible mistake. It wasn't your husband who died, it was someone else."

Dakota said, "Alexia should be here to hear this too." This jolted me back to reality. I didn't want my twenty-four-year-old daughter driving after she heard the news. The chaplain offered to contact a family member to pick up Alexia. Dakota said he'd go along to tell his sister the news in person.

When the kids returned to the house, I clung to both of them. The three of us sobbed in one another's arms. I flashed back to the countless times Todd, the kids and I had shared group hugs. I was relieved to have Dakota and Alexia with me, but it felt incomplete without Todd's muscular arms enveloping us. I kept thinking there must be some mistake; at any moment Todd would come bounding in and tell us it was all a horrible mix-up. But I couldn't deny the presence of the officer and chaplain, nor the absence of my beloved husband.

The kids and I sat in stunned silence as the officer offered us more details about the accident. He described Todd's motorcycle and how witnesses on the scene had gotten Todd's name off his driver's license from the wallet in his back pocket. Every word was like a punch to the gut that left me gasping for air.

I struggled to stay composed as the officer and the chaplain told us how to make funeral arrangements. I heard their words, but the shock made it difficult to concentrate. "Mrs. Fletcher, someone from Organ Donation will be calling you very soon," the officer said. I forced myself to focus on what he was saying. "They'll have many questions for you, and it will take a while. They have to act fast, Mrs. Fletcher. Time is a huge factor."

I thought back to a conversation I'd had with Todd and Dakota a couple of months earlier. Dakota had been at the kitchen island filling out his driver's license change of address form since we had recently moved into a new home.

"Should I check the organ donation box?" he'd asked me and Todd. We'd all shared a look.

"There's only one answer for that, son," Todd had said. He felt strongly that everyone should do their part.

Todd and I had watched as Dakota checked the box marked "Yes."

As I recalled that afternoon, it occurred to me that everything I thought about Todd from that moment on would be memories. We would never have time together as a family again. I'd never watch Todd while he cooked dinner, sit outside and gaze at the stars with him, or hear him coming in the door and calling out to me, "Hey babe, I'm home!"

Numbness set in. My body grew limp with the weight of grief. I longed for nighttime to come, wishing that I could fall asleep and later wake up from this nightmare. I'd roll over and feel Todd alongside me on the bed. I'd drape my arm across his stomach and tell him to wake up.

"I had a nightmare that you were gone, babe," I'd tell him.

He would hold me and say, "It's just a dream, honey. Go back to sleep. I've got you." He was always the one I leaned on in times of difficulty or sorrow. Todd and I had been together for thirty years, since I was sixteen and he was twenty. I'd shared my entire adult life with him. He was everything to me, the person I depended on and loved more than anyone else. I couldn't fathom living a single day without him.

The officer was saying something about identifying Todd's body at the morgue, and an autopsy. Again, his voice jolted me back to the present moment. My breath caught in my throat. I gasped at the harsh truth I couldn't ignore no matter how hard I tried. This wasn't some awful nightmare; I was never going to wake up next to my husband again.

2

THE BEST AND WORST
SUMMER

The year before Todd died had been an especially good one for us. We'd moved into our dream home in March, just four months before his accident. I looked around the house, seeing Todd in everything. The mirror we hung together above the fireplace caught my eye. Then I imagined him standing at the sink washing dishes and putting his lunch together at the kitchen counter. I even recalled the sound of him coming in the front door.

It had taken us a long time to get to our dream home. We'd raised our children on a five- acre hobby farm in Kenyon, a rural town about 60 miles from Minneapolis. The place needed a lot of work, and it seemed like we were always fixing something. Todd loved our little two-bedroom, one-bath home, but I'd always wanted more.

Over the years, I often suggested remodeling projects to update the '70s wallpaper and everything else about the house that felt dated and old. We did most of the work ourselves since we didn't have the money to hire anyone. With the help of family and friends, we'd turned the bare attic into a master suite with a walk-out deck and added a dormer with a large picture window overlooking the horses.

Todd was very content with our life there, but I couldn't shake the desire for a new home. In between improvement projects, I spent a lot of time looking at houses. I searched for listings and told Todd about the ones that caught my eye. He would indulge me and go with me to look at them, but we never found the perfect place. We were so busy working, paying down debt, and raising the kids that the time never seemed quite right to move. Eventually, I enlisted the help of my friend Becky, an intuitive medium and healer I had met in 2010 when I'd walked past the Monarch, a shop that sold crystals, jewelry and beautiful things. There was a sidewalk sign inviting people to come inside for an intuitive reading. I'd felt drawn to go inside, where Becky was seated at a little table in a quaint back room doing intuitive readings.

"What can I do for you?" Becky had asked warmly when I stepped into her space. Her soothing demeanor immediately put me at ease. The large, comfortable chairs had soft pillows on them; there were crystals and angel cards on the table and throughout the room. I smelled incense burning. Becky invited me to sit down; she asked me to give her a moment to check in with my guides and angels. She had long, thick, pitch-black hair with a few strands of blue peeking out one side, accentuating her large sparkling eyes. An attractive woman, she seemed strong, yet gentle.

She told me my angels and guides were always around me, guiding and supporting me. She connected to them and gave me their loving messages. "Your mother and grandmother are here," said Becky. I felt excited and sad at the same time. I looked around. She smiled kindly, "I can see their energy, the images they send me, hear their words."

She chuckled, "Your guides and angels are telling me you ate a lot of gum as a child."

"Yes, that is true," I said. I was surprised. It was such a random thing for her to say. How could she know that? My sister Annette and I would find change in the cushions of my grandfather's couch. He always wore big blue overalls with large pockets, and some afternoons he would take a nap, and his change would fall out. We would give grandpa back his change, but he would let us keep all the pennies. When we could, we would go uptown to the dime store and use the pennies to buy gumballs by the bagful. They tasted so good, I couldn't stop myself from swallowing them, even after my grandmother warned, "Gum will stay in your body for 7 years!"

Becky smiled and nodded, "Your grandma thought that was a good way for you to know it was her." Becky then asked me if I had any questions; I had several.

For starters, I had just been thrust into a new job as a guardian social worker for Rice County Social Services and was feeling emotional. I didn't want to leave my job as a children's mental health case manager to work with adults in guardianship, but I wasn't given a choice. The director at the county had reassigned me, and there was little I could do about it.

Becky assured me that the position would turn out to be the right one for me. She offered me guidance and positive messages from angels and guides and from my loved ones on the other side. She connected to my deceased mother and paternal grandmother and told me things no one could possibly know unless they were talking directly to them.

My fear and confusion over my job change started to lift as I listened to Becky and took notes. It was the beginning of a beautiful connection. I began meeting with her on a regular basis. I always left our sessions feeling a sense of ease, purpose and direction. I learned a lot about myself from working with her and connecting with Spirit. Over the years, Becky and I became close friends.

"Becky," I said when I called her in 2012 for advice around our living situation, "is there a house out there for us? We've been searching for such a long time."

She told me that Todd and I could manifest our dream home under a new moon.

"I'll try anything; please tell me how to do it," I pleaded. She instructed me to write down our intentions on paper and burn them outside under the new moon, then to make love as we thought about our new house. The energy and intention we focused on together would help us create our desired home.

Todd smiled and listened as I enthusiastically told him what Becky had said. He wasn't as interested in spiritual practices as I was, but he knew how badly I wanted a different home. He was willing to do the moon manifesting ritual because it was important to me. Plus, he liked how the night would end. I felt so connected to him as we wrote up a list of the things we wanted most.

"Ok, honey, thanks for doing this," I said. "Becky said we should take turns saying the things we want and write them down on a piece of paper. Under the light of the new moon, we will burn the paper while focusing on the joy and excitement of having the things we want manifest. And later after that, we make love while focusing our intentions on the love and the joy of the new home."

"Got it," he smiled as I excitedly pulled out a notepad and pen from the night stand.

"You go first honey," I said. "Well, first I'd like a lot of room for the horses, so it has to have at least the number of acres we have now or more, and a barn." We tore down the old barn just a couple of years before and put up a bigger one, so it made sense that he wanted a barn. "It would be nice if there was a creek running through it but not necessary," he said.

"Remember babe, this is a wish list, so let's put it down," I said.

"It would also be nice if it had a woodshop or man cave," he said.

I grinned, liking how he was getting into this. "I know how much you love your wood shop." Some nights he would fall asleep in the small woodshop that was just 30 feet from the backdoor. It had a wood stove, record player, stereo, and a small workbench. There was only room for Todd and maybe five of his friends to hang out in there. I'd sometimes have to go down on a weekend night and nudge him gently, "Come up to bed honey." Other times I would find him there, especially on a Sunday morning, listening to rock music. His favorite band was AC/DC.

Then it was my turn. "I really want a nice big kitchen where we can have room to cook meals together and have it open to the dining room so everyone can see each other and talk. I'd also like a porch or deck area," I said.

He smiled, "That sounds nice."

"Oh, and I want the home to be newer and updated, no more fixes." We agreed this list would make a perfect place for us and a place for the kids to come home to since Dakota was close to graduating.

Todd said, " Oh, one more thing. It needs to have a garage." We had lived through years of harsh Minnesota winters without one. "We deserve a garage," he added.

After we did the ritual, we enlisted a realtor to sell our home, contingent on us finding a house. Michelle was efficient and professional. She felt confident she could help us find the right home and told us exactly what we needed to do to stage our house for showings. We worked painstakingly throughout the summer and fall to update our house to get top dollar for it.

Becky kept telling me she saw us in a house west of the freeway in Faribault, near both of our jobs. She described the topography of the land and told me that we would be able to afford it.

In January 2013, Michelle told us about a beautiful property in Shieldsville, near Lake Mazaska. It was located west of the freeway, just like Becky had said, with the topography she'd described. The six-acre property included several sheds, a barn for the horses, a shop, and a beautiful, well-cared-for-home. It hit everything on our list except for the creek, but it was near the lake and had several garage stalls.

The moment Todd walked into the steel and knotty pine woodshop, I knew we would buy the property. His eyes lit up like a kid's on Christmas morning. The shop had a full bar, several car stalls with a drain for washing cars, and a bathroom.

I stood back and watched Todd's face as he moved about the shop. Michelle and I shared a look because we could see how much he loved it. His smile grew bigger as he walked about the space and took in everything. He kept asking me what I thought, and I kept bringing it back to him.

"Hey, you're the one who would be down here the most; what do you think?"

"This is really nice, babe. We could have our friends over, and I could fix your brakes down here." On and on he went, and that smile never left his face.

"And my sister lives a block away," Todd said to Michelle.

She smiled, "Is that a good thing?"

Todd and I both nodded our heads. "Yes, it's a great thing," Todd said. The thought of having his sister Lynn and brother-in-law Tim for neighbors was extra special to Todd.

There was a lot to see. The shop was divided into two sections; it had its own fridge, bathroom, full bar for entertaining, TV, cupboards, and furnace. There was a man cave section that seemed like a small cabin, with it's knotty pine walls; two garage stalls and a larger area with three oversize garage stalls for working on cars; and a workbench area and cupboards with large overhead lights. Basically this was more than a woodshed or man cave; it was the size of a house.

Between the outbuildings and the shop, Todd counted *nine* garage spaces, more than enough space for his cars, motorcycles, horse carts, and wagons. And I loved the house, with its large kitchen and backyard and a glass door on the main level overlooking the backyard. It was all set up for a deck to be put there at a later time.

When we told Michelle we loved the property, she said, "It just went on the market, and I think this one is going to go fast." We took her advice and asked her to call immediately with an offer.

Todd and I were preparing dinner for Alexia, Dakota, and our grandson Jackson when Michelle called. After several back-and-forth phone negotiations, we settled on a price with the sellers. I hung up the phone and announced, "We got it!" All of us jumped up and down, laughing and hugging one another. When we calmed down a bit Todd said, "Wow. Good job on the price babe. I can't believe they went down on it."

I replied, "I guess it's meant to be."

We moved into our new home on March 25, 2013. We'd finally made it. We had realized our American dream. Todd and I were giddy as we brought in our belongings. He put his arm around my shoulders as we took in our new surroundings. "You did it, babe," he said to me. "We're here because of you."

"*We* did it," I corrected him, as tears of happiness filled my eyes. "We did it together." And it felt so good, like we had it all. I imagined so many new memories were about to happen. I thought of Dakota finishing high school and having his teenage friends come hang out in the basement where there was so much room. I imagined Alexia and Jackson coming over and all the family dinners. Alexia loved cooking at the old house. She would surprise her dad with a new recipe, and Todd would go on and on about how great it was. Now we had this big beautiful kitchen with plenty of space to cook and gather.

We planned to fence the backyard for the dogs to play in, and Todd had put together plans for landscaping the backyard. More and more trees, because he loved trees.

We had four months of bliss in our new house. Time had seemed to almost stand still that summer in the few months before Todd died. He and I accomplished a lot, and we had so much fun doing it. He painted fences, made benches using the timber he had cut from trees at the old house, landscaped, and spent valuable time with family and friends.

I bought him his dream workbench, and he stayed up late at night putting it together and excitedly showing me where each tool went. "Look, babe, there's so many drawers. One for the hammers, one for drill bits and drills." He went on and on, opening the drawers one by one and saying he was going to stay really organized. I sat on the couch off and on, watching him work. He got everything put away so nicely, hung all of our pictures, and planted a bunch of trees. We spent late nights after he got home from the factory sitting in our lawn chairs, holding hands and looking at the stars.

We arranged the Adirondack chairs on the cement slab outside the entrance overlooking the backyard when we first got there. Several nights, when it was clear and comfortable, we would sit there looking at the stars, and Todd would say, "Isn't it a beautiful night? I love nights like these. I'm so glad to be here with you, honey." We would talk about our plans, the kids, and the funny things that Jackson was doing.

In hindsight, it seemed as if Todd had an endless stream of energy that summer and an urgency about getting things done and spending time with the people he loved. It was as if he was preparing for his transition. On a soul level, he took some time to tie up loose ends. He invited his parents to camp in their camper on our property during his vacation week and went fishing and played cards with them.

He even gave me permission to tear down the old red barn on the corner of the property. Weeks earlier he had told me how lovely it would be to fix it up, but right before he died he said, "On second thought, we could tear that down." I was surprised at the time, but now I believe it was his way of making sure I knew I could do what I needed; otherwise, I would have kept the barn to honor his wishes.

In the kitchen, the children and I continued to hold on tight to each other, not knowing what to do next. Eventually, the sheriff and chaplain left as family and friends arrived. I went to my bedroom periodically to escape, as more people filtered in and out of the house. At one point, my sister came into the bedroom. "Sis, how am I going to live without him, it's just not possible," I said. "I need him; the kids need him."

"I know," she managed as she hugs me tightly.

Later, my good friends Joy and Gina came into the bedroom. I could see the tears in Gina's eyes; she looked so devastated that I asked Joy if she was okay. Joy reached for my face and held my head in her hands.

I stayed a few more minutes and then rushed back into the living room to be with Alexia and Dakota, wondering how to comfort them when I didn't know how. I was so grateful to have both children with me.

I blinked back tears as vivid memories of the last four months filled my mind. Though tears blurred my surroundings, I could still make out the green LOVE sign that Alexia had bought me. Todd and Alexia had hung it on the kitchen backsplash. They loved doing small projects together. I recalled telling them exactly where I wanted it hung and how Alexia had marked the spots for Todd to drill the holes for the screws. My mind reeled with disbelief. We'd worked so hard to get into our dream house. We'd searched so long for it. Todd had touched every area of the house, and everything in it reminded me of my husband. Todd couldn't be dead; he was still all around me.

3

SEEKING SIGNS

By 7 p.m. the night of Todd's accident, exhaustion had taken over. I stepped into my bedroom, away from my sister Annette, Todd's sister Lynn, my co-worker Joy, some of my girlfriends, and Todd's parents, all of whom had gathered to support me and the kids. I desperately needed to talk to Becky.

"Becky, something terrible has happened," I said when she answered the phone. My voice shook. "Todd died today." I choked on the words. They sounded so final. "He was in an accident on his motorcycle in Northfield."

"Oh Brenda, I'm so sorry," Becky gasped. "That's why I've been seeing red-tailed hawks all day. Dozens of them have been flying in the skies here in Northfield." I was shocked because I never told her about red-tailed hawks and what they meant to Todd.

Red-tailed hawks were Todd's favorite bird. He loved those beautiful, majestic animals. At Becky's words, I thought back to a promise Todd and I had once made to each other. We were lying in bed at the house in Kenyon. It was a cold night, and we were cuddling, warming up and talking like we loved to do. This night, like other nights when it was cold, Todd had warmed up the bed for me.

When Todd and my brother worked on converting the attic into our master bedroom they didn't create enough heat ducting for the huge space. My brother Adrian said we needed to insulate around the base of the roof, but we never got around to it. Instead, we used an electric heater on the nights when it was really cold.

Occasionally, on really cold nights Todd would jump inside the covers on my side of the bed and roll around to warm it before I got in. Then he would roll over to his side of the bed and say, "Come on in, I got it warmed up for you, honey," as he patted his hand on the bed.

It was such a sweet gesture that on this night - as I often did- I got a little emotional. "I'm just going to miss you so much if one of us should die."

"Why do you think that sweetheart, it's not going to happen. You don't need to worry yourself?" he said.

"Just the same, babe, I think we need to come up with a sign so the other one knows we are okay if one of us should die. A sign to let one of us know the other is in heaven."

"Ok," said Todd. "If I die first, I will send you red-tailed hawks."

"Ahh, you love those birds."

"What sign would you send?" he asked.

"I will send you my favorite flowers, white daisies. Lots and lots of them," I answered. White daisies were our wedding flower.

The conversation had ended with me insisting that I had to die first so I wouldn't have to live without him. He'd refused to promise, saying he didn't want to live without me either. We'd settled for dying at the same time.

+ + +

"Becky, I really need to see you," I pleaded. "I have to talk to Todd." I wanted her to try and reach Todd, to give me some message from him like those she had given me from my mother and my grandmother.

Becky said two things that gave me the courage I needed to get through the night. "Brenda, Todd wants you to know how much he loves you, and he wants you to know he did not suffer." She suggested that she come to the house Friday evening so the kids and I could meet with her privately.

It was disappointing to wait two days, but with a funeral to plan and a steady stream of family and friends coming by, it was the best we could do. Becky assured me that Todd was okay and that he was watching over all of us. Deceased loved ones often send signs of their presence in an effort to communicate with us. Becky told me to look for signs from Todd that would tell me he was still with me even if I couldn't see him.

As I thought about what meeting with Becky would be like for me and the kids, I struggled with the notion of never holding my husband again, never feeling him, seeing him, or hearing him. Never had I felt this much pain and desperation. My heart felt crushed. I held my stomach, feeling I would literally fall to pieces if I didn't physically hold myself together.

I had experienced my first loss at age 12 when my maternal grandmother Myra, my protector and safe haven, died of cancer. Grandma had passed away in a nursing home with her husband, children, and sisters around her. She'd told everyone how much she loved them and then rolled over and said, "I'm going to heaven now," as she closed her eyes. Grandma knew she was going home. Todd died on the pavement surrounded by strangers. I would have given anything to have been there with him.

After my grandmother's death, I felt so afraid of life until I met Todd. I was very close to my grandma. She accepted and revered me. She kept me safe when she could, when my mom wasn't able to, at no real fault of her own.

Life seemed so scary and confusing. The chaos at home stayed with me even when I wasn't there. I would often daydream in school about fixing the things that were wrong, but I really didn't know how to make things better. When I had quiet talks with Grandma, I felt supported, loved and valued.

After I grew up, I knew that my mom wanted to be there for me, but she couldn't. I was angry with her at times, but deep down I knew she couldn't help it. Her schizophrenia kept her from being there the way she and I wanted her to be. Even at a young age, I knew that. After I had children of my own, I appreciated her more and more. The love and kindness she had shown me must have been tough for her as she was trying to just to survive.

My second major loss was my mom. I lost her to cancer in 2008, and I couldn't imagine life without her. Todd was my rock, steadfastly helping me get through my grief. Mom and I had grown closer as I was an adult with children of my own. I was amazed by her strength, getting through her abusive childhood and marriage. She was full of love for herself, her family, and for Jesus. We often talked about religion and spirituality, having different views but a lot of similar core beliefs. I still miss her dearly.

It was hard losing my mom and grandma. But as deeply as those losses were felt, they were nothing compared to what I felt at Todd's passing. Losing my husband was like losing part of my soul. Despair flooded me, took my breath away. I needed Todd. Without him I was incomplete. For thirty years our lives had intertwined, and I had thrived on the love and attention he showed me daily. Being with him made me a better version of myself. I couldn't begin to imagine who I'd be without him. As these thoughts grew into a wave of grief and terror that threatened to drown me, I grabbed onto the hope that Becky could communicate with Todd. I just had to make it until Friday.

Getting through that first night felt like it would take a miracle. Every part of me ached for my husband. I felt so alone. I was desperate to feel Todd's presence. I wondered where he was. I believed in some kind of heaven, but I'd also heard that sometimes when people died they remained near their loved ones. I ached for some sign from Todd that would assure me he was there, even if I couldn't see or hear him.

Eventually my family and friends left. Alexia stayed overnight. We lay in my bed, holding each other. The phone rang, and for a moment I thought it was Todd, calling on his break at work. I spent the seemingly endless hours before daylight lost in thought. What if I'd lingered longer this morning? Would Todd still be alive then? What if I'd responded to the text he'd sent me before he went to run errands? He would have left a moment later, and he might still be here. A single moment could have changed everything.

I decided to listen to his voice messages on my phone. "Hi beautiful, figured since I couldn't tuck you in, at least I could call and hear your voice. Love you, sweetheart."

I recalled how I'd waited up for Todd to get home the night before. I'd heard the roar of his motorcycle coming closer to the house and grinned with the anticipation of talking with him and kissing him. I met him outside by the garage and told him about some benches I had seen at Menards.

"Don't you have enough benches, Sweetie?" he'd teased.

"Of course not," I'd replied. "You can never have enough benches, they're like shoes."

He'd debated whether he should get the overspray on his bike fixed. We walked down to the shop so he could show it to me. I told him I could hardly see the overspray.

"It shouldn't be there...it should be fixed, shouldn't it?" he said. Todd wasn't always the most organized person, but he was meticulous about the things that mattered to him, including his bike.

We'd walked up from the shop and stood by the young maple tree next to the garage. It was the kind of night where I could have stayed up and watched the stars with him, but I'd felt tired and decided to go up to the house. Todd had said he would be up soon.

"I love you, babe; see you in a bit," he called as I headed to the house. I watched Craig Ferguson for a short time, but I went to bed before Todd came in. Now I wished I'd stayed awake. I'd give anything to turn back the clock and have more time with Todd.

4

THE LOVE OF MY LIFE

I've heard that when people die, they go through a life review, reliving all the experiences of their lifetime and what they felt during those events. They also feel the impact their lives had on others. People who have had near-death experiences report going through a similar process.

The day Todd died, I spent half the night caught up in my own life review, reliving the big events like our wedding, the births of our children, and the recent move into our dream house, but savoring even more the quieter moments of our daily life. I was grateful for every single one and took solace in recalling all the precious memories we had made in our time together.

Todd and I met at a party in the summer of 1983. I saw him at a few gatherings, and by the end of the summer, I had a crush on him. My friend Kathy did some investigating and found out Todd was interested in me, too. She arranged a double date at the drive-in movies with her and her boyfriend. I don't remember the movie, just my overwhelming insecurity.

I didn't say a word the entire night. I was so painfully shy I clutched the car door handle in an effort to calm my nerves. I could only nod and smile as Todd tried valiantly to make conversation.

The next day, Kathy came over for a debriefing. She shook her head at my crippling anxiety. "You could have at least talked to the poor guy," she teased.

It was hard to believe Todd wanted to see me again, but thank God he did. I lived a couple of blocks from Main Street and usually walked down there several times a day. Todd drove around town in his green 1972 Chevrolet Chevelle, cruising the streets looking for his friends or just passing time. Whenever he drove by, he'd flash me the peace sign, his right hand stretched out along the dash. Eventually, we went on long drives and talked for hours. We became friends, and Todd taught me how to drive.

That fall, I began my junior year of high school. Todd often picked me up after his shift at a production company ended at midnight, and we drove around, talking into the early morning hours. He'd ask if he should take me home since I had school the next day, but I always wanted to stay with him. I often nodded off in class from my late-night running around, but I didn't care. I loved being with Todd more than anything. I could be myself around him. He made me feel secure, worthy, and loved—feelings I hadn't felt since my grandmother Myra had died.

Todd offered me respite from the unpredictability of my home life. I lived with my parents, two brothers, and sister in a little white house on Home Street in Kenyon, Minnesota. Life in our house was filled with chaos and drama. Both of my parents struggled with mental illness, my mother with schizophrenia and my father with bipolar disorder. Both were often hospitalized, though rarely at the same time. We got by on welfare and food stamps since neither of my parents could work. My oldest brother Adrian and my sister Annette were like parents to me; they helped me navigate life in my parents' frequent absences.

I remember making visits to the state hospital. I always stayed close to my brother or sister. I was afraid of the other patients as we walked down the halls. I can still see the pain in their eyes. Some of them crouched in corners. Others yelled and screamed.

"You're okay, Brenda," my brother Adrian always reassured me. He protected me and my sister when we were scared. I didn't understand a lot at the time. I just knew I wished to be anywhere but there.

I never felt like I fit into my family, our town, or anywhere in the world. I knew we lived differently from other people. I felt afraid most of the time. Early on, I learned to be the good kid, the quiet one. I tried my best to stay on the sideline, unnoticed, looking for ways to stop potential crisis situations at home.

I didn't want to cause any trouble in an already stressful world. So, I learned to adapt and cope, to stay calm, and to hide from my father's rages when necessary. Dad was emotionally abusive and prone to tirades. He screamed at us kids and shook his fist, telling us we would never amount to anything. But it was his physical and emotional abuse of my mother that left the most scarring on my soul.

My mother was religious and kind. She loved to write songs and sing about her love for Jesus. She didn't know how to get her own needs met, much less how to parent. She had gone from growing up in a physically abusive home to being abused by the words and hands of my father. At her sickest, she would run around the house screaming and spitting into pots and pans, trying to get the "demons" out of her body. In better times, she would wash our feet with a washcloth and a bucket of soapy water like she said Jesus did for his disciples.

I remember the late nights I'd come home after being out with Todd and our friends.

"Brenda, is that you?" My mom would call out. "Can I make you something to eat?"

"No, mom, I'm fine," I would shout back. She would often get up, even if it was 3 a.m., to cook me something (usually french fries) whether I ate it or not. It took years before I really felt a deep appreciation for her caring ways.

In my late teens and twenties, I struggled to define myself apart from the roles I held in my family. I longed for peace from the constant chatter in my brain telling me I wasn't good enough and would never amount to much — tapes of my father's voice that played in my head. I'd hear him telling me he wished I had never been born and that I was stupid and ungrateful for everything he did for me.

I had also absorbed all the hurtful things he said to my mom and my siblings. I'd taken all his harsh criticism in, and it continued to hurt me. I spent my childhood and early teenage years trying to figure out how I could be better, be worthy.

The first few years Todd and I were together, I repeatedly pushed him away. Part of me wondered what would happen when he discovered who I truly was. I created confusion and drama because upset was familiar to me. Crisis felt normal. I was an explosion of complicated emotions, quick to anger for no reason. I was unsettled and unsure about everything, introverted and reserved.

Todd, on the other hand, was a free spirit, full of happiness, humor, compassion and love. To Todd, family was everything. He came from a very traditional home. His mother raised him and his four siblings, and his dad worked in a factory. They lived on a farm. Todd respected his parents and their strong work ethic.

While the peace I felt when I was with Todd made me feel good, it was also uncomfortable. I was surprised and confused by his willingness to accept me unconditionally. I questioned his love for me. Todd kept loving me exactly as I was. He saw the best in me no matter my mood. I wanted to be a better person. I wanted to be the kind of woman who deserved a man like Todd. He was always easy to get along with and easy to love. I appreciated that about him more and more over the years, especially in difficult times, like when I unexpectedly became pregnant.

When the nurse in the clinic told us we were expecting, I started crying. I was just twenty-two years old, hardly an adult. I knew nothing about being a good partner in a relationship or how to be a successful parent.

Todd held me and grinned. "Babe, it's going to be so great," he said. "You're going to be a great mom; I know it."

I looked around the tiny exam room, feeling like my world was suddenly getting very small. The walls seemed to be closing in. Then Todd said something that eased my fear. "We're in this together, babe." He teared up, and we held each other tight. I managed a small smile.

The nurse grinned as she said to me, "It looks like you have a lot of support here."

Todd's love and support never wavered over the years. If anything, it grew stronger. When our son Dakota was diagnosed with cystic fibrosis, a chronic illness primarily affecting the lungs, I remember feeling devastated and crying a lot with Todd. We blamed ourselves.

We feared the extra load our son would have to carry through life. Todd was determined to do everything he could to help Dakota stay strong and healthy. He managed our son's medical care and treatment, making sure Dakota took his medications, got to doctors' appointments, and did his therapies. I was relieved at how Todd organized this part of our lives. It was overwhelming for both of us, but he was always my rock. I couldn't imagine how I'd manage without him.

5

DAISIES ARE A
HAPPY FLOWER

A few times during that first night after Todd died, I walked downstairs to Dakota's room to check on him. Once, I spotted a framed picture of Todd and the kids on a road trip to South Dakota, sitting on the shelf that lined the basement steps. Alexia had given it to her dad a few years earlier for Father's Day. I picked up the picture and drank in the image of Todd joyfully hugging the kids. My eyes were practically swollen shut from crying, but more tears came.

As I headed back to my bedroom, a Sunday afternoon from a couple of years earlier popped into my head. Todd had been in the barn with his team of Belgian horses, Ellie and Mae, pulling together the tack for a wagon ride. I'd been doing things in the house and decided to see what he was up to outside. I loved watching him do tasks that excited him, like working with the horses.

Todd's face lit up when he saw me. He reached for a folding chair from the corner of the barn, unfolded it, and set it next to him near the horses. "Have a seat, my love. I love it when you come out here. You don't have to help me; I just love it when you're nearby."

He made me feel loved. I don't know how a person can really feel at ease without it. I believe there is a dedicated place in the heart reserved for the person who gets you like no one else. Someone who loves you on the same level. Where your heart feels so comfortable and settled, and you know it's where you belong; where nothing could ever come between the two of you because you understand each other on a soul level. Todd is that to me.

Even after all these years, he still got excited when I walked into a room. The length of our relationship hadn't dampened our affection for one another. Our mutual love and respect had grown stronger with every experience that we made into shared memories.

I always felt like Todd put me and the kids first. He worked hard and took pride in providing for us. He didn't always like his job, but he rarely complained about it. In his spare time, he rode his horses and his motorcycle and went fishing with his friends. Todd and I had different hobbies and interests, but our love and our family were our most important priorities. I never questioned Todd's devotion. I was number one in his heart, and he was number one in mine.

On special occasions and holidays, Todd would often put daisies on my nightstand. He wanted them to be the first things I saw when I woke in the morning. Simple and sweet, daisies are a happy flower. They last a really long time. I even like when the petals fall off and lie around the vase. I knew how lucky I was, and I tried to never take my husband for granted. The night after the accident, I yearned to tell him I loved him and that I couldn't live without him. I wished I could have done something different and kept him from leaving that day. It was too soon for him to go. The kids and I needed him. I was desperate to get him back.

It occurred to me that denial could serve a very useful purpose, allowing me to find my way to acceptance as slowly as I needed. Tragedy needs to be absorbed and processed slowly for a reason. The hope of Todd returning was like a life raft keeping me just above the water so I could get from one day to the next.

At some point before first light, I crept back into bed, careful not to wake Alexia, who was asleep next to me where Todd usually slept. Despite seeing my daughter there instead of my husband, I couldn't fathom life without Todd at my side.

6

STEPS

A stream of friends and family passed through the house in the days between Todd's death and his funeral. I was surrounded with love and support and grateful for it, but unable to feel much of the love because of the unbearable pain of my loss. Todd's steady reassurance was the only thing I wanted and needed, the only thing I couldn't have now that he was gone.

The visitors were a welcome distraction, but I felt I had only one shot to get the service right, and I wanted to focus on the preparations. Todd was an amazing man who deserved the best funeral I could give him. I owed him that and so much more.

There were many decisions to make, including some that seemed impossible and cruel. I had to decide if I wanted to view the body. *Todd's body.* The arms that had once wrapped around me. The smile that drew me in. The hands that held me tight. The body that harbored the soul of the man I loved more than life itself.

It was a very important decision. I would only get one opportunity. I worried that I would regret it if I didn't see him one last time, then feared I'd regret it if I did. Maybe seeing Todd's still form would help me accept his death. But I wasn't sure I wanted to remember him that way, not when I had so many vibrant, lively memories of him.

After much thought, I decided to forego the viewing. Dakota also chose not to go. Alexia went to say a final goodbye to her father with Todd's parents and sister. I wish I could have been there for my daughter, but I just couldn't. I spent those couple of days racing around the house gathering photographs for collages to display at the funeral home, writing a love letter to Todd for Alexia to read on my behalf at the service, and finding the perfect songs to reflect Todd. Keeping busy meant I didn't have to confront the grief and loss that threatened to overwhelm me every time I slowed down.

I was running around in a mild frenzy when my friend Vicki stopped me. It was the first time she'd been in our new home. She took my hand and led me into the bathroom, the only quiet area of the house. With tears in her eyes, she told me she could see I needed to step away from everyone for just a moment. She stood in the bathroom with me, and we took a deep breath together. "Brenda, I could feel the love in your house the moment I walked in the door," she said as she hugged me.

We talked briefly about how the love wouldn't go away just because Todd had died. It was exactly what I needed to hear. I was so caught up in my anguish. I needed connection with his love, needed to know it wasn't lost.

I counted the hours until Becky's visit Friday evening. If I could just make it until she arrived, Becky would help me communicate with Todd. All the memories I'd been calling up were a balm to my sorrow, but I was frantic for a stronger connection to my husband. I missed his kisses, his warm embraces, even the smell of him. I ached for Todd. I barely held on throughout the day Friday as I watched the minutes tick by painfully slowly.

Finally, it was Friday night. Becky brought me a beautiful necklace she'd made, a pair of silver angel wings. "Todd wants you to know he is always with you," she whispered as she clasped the necklace around my neck. I nodded, too choked up to answer.

I'd asked Alexia and Dakota to talk with Becky too. Alexia understood. We'd had many conversations about spirituality over the years. She knew how much the meeting with Becky meant to me, and she wanted answers too. Dakota had always been skeptical. He agreed to the meeting if it was brief, saying, "I'll do it for you, Mom."

People had gathered in the kitchen and the living room, so I took Becky downstairs to the finished basement. She sat on one of the chairs looking out over the backyard. Dakota was outside playing badminton with some classmates. I called him to join us, and he reluctantly came inside and joined me and Alexia on the couch.

As we all settled in, Becky grew silent. She drew outlines in the air with her fingers, something I had seen her do numerous times throughout the years. I've never asked why she draws in the air, but it's always followed by a message from the other side. I came to know that she does this as her way to connect with Spirit. "Spirit" is a term that includes anyone who has passed on from earth, as well as our angels and guides.

Kim Russo, accomplished medium and author known as "the Happy Medium," describes angels as "Celestial, spiritual beings, superior to humans in power and intelligence." She says, "Angels are made up of pure light of the God force and were created by God to serve as his helpers to humanity, as well as to help serve the heavenly realm." Russo describes spirit guides as "human souls who have lived on the earth at one time and have crossed over into the light."

We all have guides and angels around us at all times, even though most of us aren't open to seeing them. We can ask for their help and guidance. Our loved ones who have passed over can visit us anytime, even though we humans may have difficulty connecting to them.

"Todd says he's sitting on the basement steps," Becky announced.

My eyes flew toward the carpeted steps. *Empty.* I squinted hard, trying to force myself to see Todd sitting there.

"He used to sit on the steps as a child and listen to his parents. He says you can ask him anything. He is always with you," Becky relayed. I imagined Todd as a little boy sitting on the steps in his family home, a time in his life I didn't know much about. I longed to be sitting there alongside him, just the two of us, the way we used to sit together and talk.

Dakota started crying. Alexia and I started crying too.

"Todd is telling you it's like the Aerosmith song, *I Don't Want to Miss a Thing*," Becky continued. "He's saying, 'I'll be with all of you always.'"

Fixated on the senselessness of Todd's departure, I was about to ask Becky why Todd had been taken from us so abruptly when my sister Annette opened the basement door.

"Brenda, I'm sorry to bother you, but the funeral home director needs to talk with you. They have to do the cremation soon."

I jumped up and walked over toward the basement steps. "Sis, I told you I don't want to be disturbed while Becky is here." I fought to curb my frustration at the interruption. I didn't care if the rest of the world disappeared. I just wanted to be left alone with Becky and the kids so we could hear from Todd. I had so many things to ask him.

"I'm sorry, but the funeral home director needs to speak with you," Annette insisted.

"Remember, I'm in this meeting now. I told you, I don't want to be disturbed. I'll talk to him after I'm finished." Nothing mattered more to me than communicating with Todd.

Annette looked worried, but she nodded and went back upstairs. I had waited so long for Becky to confirm that Todd was indeed in heaven and was communicating with me. Even though I knew she would connect with him, I was struck with doubt. What if there was no such thing as an afterlife or heaven? What if Todd was truly gone, and I could never talk to him again?

My doubt faded as Becky brought forward messages from Todd. The words sounded so much like my husband's, I was certain she was talking with him. Becky made more tracings in the air, then told us there were lessons in Todd's passing. She said, "He's saying this doesn't make sense right now, but someday it will. You will all grow from this, Brenda. So will Todd's family and friends. Even the driver of the semi-truck."

This reminded me of something my brother Adrian used to say about Grandma Myra. He used to tell me that our grandmother had always talked about how in heaven everything will make sense even though it didn't in the moment. For our grandmother, that's where faith came in. I understood what Todd was trying to say, but I couldn't help feeling cheated. I didn't care about any lessons. I just wanted the other half of me back so I could feel whole again.

Through Becky, Todd told Dakota that he was sorry for the times he'd been hard on him and he'd done the best he could to be a good father. He also told Dakota he was so proud to be his dad and that Dakota was a wonderful son and person. Dakota's thin frame shuddered with sobs. When they subsided, we hugged, and he went back outside to be with his friends.

I worried about how my eighteen-year-old would handle life without his dad. Dakota was on the cusp of becoming a man. He needed his father, someone he could pattern his own life after and go to for male guidance and wisdom. I couldn't possibly fill in for all the ways Todd had been present in Dakota's life.

After Dakota left, Becky turned to Alexia. "Todd is asking me to tell you that you're an amazing mom to Jackson and that he's loved watching you grow into such a beautiful woman." Becky paused as if listening to something I couldn't hear. "He's saying that your psychic abilities are going to increase; there's a lot of learning and opportunity ahead for you."

"I just want Dad back," Alexia choked out, tears streaming down her face. I tried to wipe them for her, and she held my hand. I'd give anything to ease my kids' pain and make their lives better, but I couldn't give them the one thing they wanted and needed the most—their father.

Becky shifted her attention to me. "Todd says he will always be with you, Brenda," she began softly. Her words were tinged with compassion. "You can connect to him any time. He says you're the most amazing, loving wife anyone could ever dream of. He says loving you was so easy. You made everything easy. He says he didn't want to leave and was angry at first, but he's in a beautiful place with relatives, surrounded by love. Unconditional love."

In the past several years, Todd and I had often said, "I love you, babe, unconditionally," to each other. It became a little saying of ours. We had talked about the meaning of unconditional love.

Some people say that you can't love a spouse unconditionally, the way a parent loves a child. I believe that marriage has certain conditions placed on it, but love does not. No matter what we say or do, whether we cause pain or do things that dissolve a marriage, the love we've felt is real and can't be taken away. Therefore it is unconditional. When we love someone, we acknowledge their divinity, their soul. The pain we cause, the judgment and conditions we place on one another that keep us apart are all part of our humanness, our flawed selves. But love itself is spiritual, unconditional. Hearing the words unconditional love was further confirmation it was really Todd.

I wiped away tears, trying to take in everything Becky was saying. I felt grateful that Todd was with his deceased aunts and uncles, and especially his sister Kay, who had died just a few years earlier.

"It's hard for Todd to see all of you in such pain," Becky went on. She explained that Todd hadn't suffered or felt any pain when he died. Spirit took his spirit right before the impact. I had been so worried about him lying there suffering while he faded away. According to Becky, after the accident, Todd watched the people gathered around his lifeless body.

He found his way back to our house and was pleased that he was able to do that so quickly. He'd been there when the sheriff knocked at the door. Todd's spirit had entered the house and rested in the hall between the kitchen and the living room, next to a picture of the sunset that we had bought as a souvenir on our only plane trip together just a few years earlier.

We'd gone to Las Vegas and had so much fun. A street artist had spray-painted the picture, and Todd later surprised me by getting it framed for my birthday.

Becky said Todd's spirit had stood there and watched us all that first day, feeling such love for us and for his life. He'd wanted so badly to hold us as we grieved. I can't possibly relate how good it felt to hear those words from Todd. I was so grateful that he was okay, and that he was still with us. I told him how much I loved him and that I appreciated everything he did for us.

It grew late. Becky stayed while I said goodbye to our remaining friends and family. I thanked Annette for understanding that I'd wanted so badly to talk to Becky and have Todd talk through her. My sister and I had different religious beliefs, but we'd always felt free to express our opinions to one another. Despite the doubt in her eyes, she hugged me and told me she loved me.

After everyone was gone, Becky, Dakota, Alexia, and I sat at the kitchen table talking a little while longer. Suddenly the lights over the dining room table flickered.

Becky grinned. "Todd is saying he'll give you signs like that to let you know he's here."

I was certain it was Todd, but Dakota looked unconvinced. Becky said she could see Todd's energy, and that everyone has a unique color to their energy field, like a signature or a fingerprint. I felt jealous. I was glad to have Becky to act as a medium, but I wanted to hear Todd speak and to see him the way she did. Surely if she could do so, I could too. I vowed to learn as soon as possible. I'd give anything to be with my husband again any way I could.

7

A STRING OF PEARLS

There were so many people at the visitation on Saturday that the line at the funeral home seemed endless. My husband had touched a lot of lives, and we were there for hours. I hadn't seen some of the people who came to pay their respects in years. Todd's friends told me stories they remembered about him. Red, the best man at our wedding, gave me the biggest hug. I don't recall ever hugging him before throughout the years, not even at our wedding.

I could tell that Red and Todd's other close buddies were hurting a lot. Todd had been planning to go on a weekend fishing trip with several of them that weekend. Instead, they were bidding farewell to their friend. It was difficult for all of us to comprehend.

When my coworker Joy stepped forward to offer her condolences, she reminded me of one day when we were at work, and a county attorney came into the office. Joy and another colleague, Gina, introduced me to him. At one point in the conversation Gina had commented, "Brenda really likes her husband."

"Well, I should hope she likes her husband. Otherwise, why would she have married him?" the lawyer retorted.

Gina said, "No, you don't understand; she *really* likes her husband." My coworkers told the lawyer about our marriage, how the love between Todd and I had grown instead of dimming over the years.

My sister Annette, who worked at the same company as Todd, was telling everyone who would listen how Todd would find her on work breaks and say, "Brenda needs a break and some sister time. You two should go to the movies." He was always thinking of ways to make my life better.

Disbelief, shock, and sadness filled people's eyes as they wished Alexia, Dakota, and me blessings. Almost everyone who came to the wake said they would never forget Todd's laughter and how much he loved life. It was almost more than we could bear, but somehow we got through the day. We had to.

The next morning, I rose with the sun after a sleepless night. I dreaded what the day held, dreaded saying farewell to my husband, my best friend. I dressed in a simple green blouse and a knee-length skirt. I wept as Dakota helped me fasten a string of pearls around my neck.

Shortly before my 18th birthday, my golden birthday, Todd and I had been cruising around town in his car when "Pearl Necklace" by ZZ Top came on the radio. We were singing along when Todd asked me, "Do you want a pearl necklace?"

"What girl wouldn't want a pearl necklace?" I joked.

A few weeks later, Todd gave me the string of pearls for my birthday, along with five birthday cards. When I asked him why so many cards, he said he couldn't choose between them, so he'd bought them all. He baked me two birthday cakes and invited all of our friends and our siblings to his house for a surprise celebration. He made me feel so special.

When Todd had told me he loved me and wanted to be with me forever, I finally felt I belonged in the world. There were so many times my parents forgot my birthday. Even though I knew it wasn't true, I couldn't help but think that they didn't care about me. It wasn't until I was older that I understood their struggles with mental illness. Todd's attention and affection healed all the disappointments of past birthdays.

I stroked the pearls. I couldn't have imagined back then that we would ever reach an endpoint, and certainly not in such an awful way. I lifted the pearls to my mouth and kissed them in silent blessing to Todd. They would give me fortitude for what lay ahead.

I remember looking out the car window as my friend Kathy drove me to the church for the funeral. It was a sunny summer day, a beautiful day to be outside. The kind of day Todd loved the most. If he'd been alive, he would have been the one cooking breakfast before going fishing out on the lake with all of his buddies.

As Kathy drove to the service, we passed men mowing their lawns, women pushing strollers, and kids riding their bikes. For most people, it was a typical Sunday. For me, it was the final send-off for the man who'd been my everything.

At the service, Alexia read a portion of a letter Todd had written to me several years earlier. There was a particular sentence that summed up the way he viewed me. He said, "Babe, you are nature's true beauty." He was always saying beautiful things like that to me.

Alexia also read the love letter I had written to Todd. She did such an amazing job, fighting back tears, to deliver it flawlessly for me. As I listened to my daughter in the church, I wondered how I would get through the remainder of my days. I had experienced pain, loss, and heartbreak before, but losing my husband was different. I wondered if I would ever feel normal or whole again.

After the service, people came to our house. We served food in Todd's shop. My family had brought back all of the lovely flower arrangements from the funeral home. I looked through them and picked out three to keep, then invited my family and friends to take the rest. My grandson Jackson got out his toys and played. He wanted all of Todd's favorite candies, which we had out on the tables in the old-fashioned root beer mugs Todd collected. I got through the day but wanted only to lay in bed, cry, and hopefully drift off to sleep. Maybe if I closed my eyes, I could find Todd in my sleep. Somewhere in my dreams.

When I finally went into the bedroom, I was dismayed to discover the flower arrangements various family members had stored there and forgotten to take home. Alexia moved the flowers to another room and tucked me in. I told her how grateful I was to have her for a daughter and how proud I was of how she'd handled everything at the funeral. Dakota came in and hugged me.

After the kids left, I lay wide awake, staring at the ceiling, wishing I could sleep forever. Nothing could have prepared me for Todd's death. Even so, I'd had some premonition that we would one day be separated. Over the years, I sometimes said to him in bed at night, "Todd, I'm going to miss you, babe."

"I'm right here!" he'd say.

"Yes, but someday one of us will die," I'd remind him. "I'll miss you so much when that happens."

Todd always told me not to worry, but I usually cried myself to sleep those nights. He couldn't understand the anxiety I had about death, but he always comforted me. "Lay your head on my shoulder and let it pass," he said.

My greatest fear had become my reality. Todd was dead. We were no longer physically together. As I searched for a way to make sense of my loss, I felt shattered into a billion pieces. But the world around me was still going on. My family needed me. I was still living and breathing, even if I felt broken. I had to figure out how to put myself back together. While I would have given anything to go with Todd, I still needed to function in the world. My family needed me.

8

A BODY OF PAIN

After Todd's death, I felt like I was between two lives. There was my life before July 24th, 2013, and my life after. I had my foot in both worlds. Life narrowed to simply getting through each day. The weeks following the funeral were the most excruciating. I needed a way to survive from one minute to the next.

I'd taken a few weeks off from work, but once the funeral was over and I no longer had that to focus on, I had to keep busy, so I wouldn't crumble or explode. Without a regular work schedule, time seemed slippery. I'd find myself surprised by how the day seemed to turn to nighttime with no warning. I dreaded going to bed and lying next to that empty space that reminded me of everything I'd lost.

As weeks turned into months, I moved into taskmaster mode, keeping myself constantly occupied. I couldn't let myself slow down. Staying busy kept me just sane enough to function. Thoughts of Todd were unrelenting. There were so many things to do; getting copies of the death certificate, changing our assets and bills into my name, and taking care of the myriad things that needed attention on our property, like putting a fence in the backyard for our dogs.

There were the tasks that Todd had done every day, like tending his beautiful Belgian horses, Ellie and Mae, and Carmel and Abby the ponies. Whenever I walked out to the barn to feed the horses, they looked as confused as I felt. They were wondering where Todd was, too.

The level of intense physical pain that accompanied my grief surprised me. It was like being punched repeatedly. Sometimes the pain was so heavy I found myself holding my breath. The shock and disbelief I held compressed so tightly in my body made it hard for me to breathe. I'd wind up gasping for air. I had to remind myself to inhale and exhale. I was mentally and physically exhausted. Even though I lost weight, I felt weighed down. Sometimes my body felt like excess baggage. Some mornings I had to use my hands to physically lift my legs over the side of the bed.

Becky taught me to notice *where* in my body I felt pain, to acknowledge it and breathe through it until it left, or at least lessened. Most of the time, I was tempted to ignore the pain. But I learned it was crucial to feel my emotions and let them go whenever possible.

Todd and I used to lie in bed talking. Minutes melted into hours. He had this way of getting me to express everything that was going on with me. "You've got to get it off your chest, babe," he would tell me. It makes so much sense. Our chests are where our hearts are housed. We heal by feeling, experiencing, and sharing our emotions. We have to get the emotions out of our hearts. When we don't process our feelings, they build up in our bodies. I would pour my heart out to Todd and sometimes end with a good cry. He would say tenderly, "Lay your head on my shoulder." The sweetness of those words always made me cry a little more.

Todd was right, I did need to get it off my chest. I decided early on that I would survive the grief. I decided to take that advice from him and talk about my sorrow when I could. I would do my best to "get my feelings off my chest." I needed to get the pain out of my body. I needed healing in my heart. I talked to friends and family, those whom I knew would really listen. That was healing.

I also joined a grief support group, where I learned just how damaging repressed emotions can be. I heard stories of widows gambling away life savings or abusing alcohol. Processing emotions is much healthier than turning to coping mechanisms like overeating, drinking alcohol, and other reckless behaviors.

Repressed emotions can lead to chronic depression and disease. I knew this before, but now I had a deeper understanding of just how easily those things can happen after significant trauma. I could have easily buried myself in a mountain of pain. There were moments when I was so mired in grief that I couldn't see any way out. The more I held those painful feelings tightly in my heart, the more my mind filled with chatter. The noise grew louder and louder in an attempt to keep me from the pain lodged deep inside. Nothing about my life would ever be the same.

The heaviness of my dark thoughts and feelings and the permanence of the situation pinned me down. Time seemed irrelevant. Sometimes I'd let myself lay on the couch and cry, but only for a little while. Then I'd get up and start on the tasks again. I had to be vigilant about not letting my grief consume me.

Along with the pain and heartache came exhaustion and sleeplessness. I went outside several times most nights and stared at the sky in disbelief. *This can't be real. This can't be happening.* I moved from one stage of grieving into another as my denial ebbed into acceptance for a moment or two, and then denial rushed right back in again.

I was a widow at forty-six. The world and everything about it seemed cruel. I tried to compartmentalize my days to attempt to lessen the stress of it all. Regardless of what I was doing, much of the time I was lost in reverie, brooding over special moments with my husband. I remembered simple things, like Todd leaving the screen door open so I could hear the toads in the small pond we'd made below the deck of our master bedroom. I'd be lying in bed, and he would say, "Toady is making noises tonight. I'll open the screen door wider so you can hear him, babe."

The memories were both balm and curse. While they brought so much gratitude, they were a stark reminder of the gaping loss in my life. Many nights when I took our dogs out for a walk, I'd look up at the sky and beg God for answers. I couldn't make sense of any kind of divine order in Todd's death when we had been so happy together. Somewhere along the way, I realized that in remembering, I was actually reliving those moments. I could close my eyes, and it felt like Todd was there with me. I began to rely on this as a way to connect with him.

9

SIGNS FROM BEYOND

One day, I recalled what Becky had said about Todd sending me signs of his presence. I began seeing signs daily. They made me feel close to him. A few years prior to Todd's passing, I'd learned that angels and guides communicate with us through signs and numbers.

I have used angel card interpretations for a while. I'd often notice the number sequence 555 just before something significant occurred. Some intuitives believe that 555 signals significant change. The change isn't necessarily good or bad, but I discovered that whenever I saw the number 555 repeatedly, it meant something difficult was going to happen.

For instance, I kept seeing 555 when our dog Ruby needed to pass. Another time I saw it over and over again just before Dakota became very sick with complications from cystic fibrosis. Eventually I recognized that when those numbers came up, I needed to prepare for something big to happen.

I'd seen 555 everywhere prior to Todd's passing. It had made me anxious. I'd wondered why it was showing up when we had just moved into our dream house, and things were going so well. I had a gnawing fear in the pit of my stomach that something awful was going to happen. I'd tried to trust that the change could be positive, but the fear wouldn't go away. After Todd's accident, I understood the meaning of the numbers.

My angels and guides also sent me frequent 5 and 7 combinations, like 557 or 755. These combinations have always brought positive messages. After Todd passed, I saw 7's and 5's everywhere—on license plates and clocks, especially, but also in street addresses and on signs, even in the most unexpected places. Becky said Todd was sending me 5's and 7's so I'd know he was okay. He also wanted me to be aware of my thoughts when I saw the numbers. It would be confirmation about what I was thinking about. For instance, I would find myself thinking of a certain solution to a problem, and then I would see a sign like 577. I knew it was Todd telling me that was the right decision.

Todd had always carried a red handkerchief in his pocket. He'd worn it as a bandana when he was riding his motorcycle. Once when I was getting a reading from Becky, she'd chuckled and said, "Todd is saying, 'You're still using my red handkerchief, the one I left on my nightstand. You keep it on your nightstand, and you haven't washed it yet.'" Every night I cried into that red bandana handkerchief.

One night, I said a silent prayer to Todd, and then went looking for a sign from him to help me feel better. I was going through his dresser drawer when I found the two necklaces I bought for us when we first dated. Each one held half of a mizpah coin. Todd had worn his every day until it turned his neck green. I'd forgotten that he still had them.

When I laid the two halves alongside one another, they made a complete circle with an inscription:

> *The Lord watch between*
> *me and thee while*
> *we are absent*
> *one from another*

What a beautiful sign. The necklaces reminded me that despite physical separation, Todd and I are connected forever. I could practically hear my husband whispering in my ear, reminding me that not even death could keep us apart.

Todd's work pants caught my eye. They were still draped over the bottom frame of our bed. I hadn't been able to bring myself to move them. I stepped over to the bed and picked them up. Todd's scent filled my nostrils, and I breathed in deeply, greedily, as if I could conjure him up by sheer will. Todd didn't appear, but the lights blinked slowly on and off three times. I was nowhere near the switch. I knew Todd was sending me another sign: I—love—you. This happened on a few other occasions, usually when I needed it the most.

The real healing began when I started talking more frequently to Todd. I knew he was listening, but I wanted so badly to see him and hear him. I started writing him letters at the end of the day. This helped me process my grief and find ways to continue connecting with Todd.

Then there was Becky. I'd spoken with her countless times since Todd died. She always found time to speak with Todd, and her messages from him brought me tremendous solace. I wasn't able to see my husband, but talking to him through Becky was the next best thing. It gave me hope that I, too, could learn to communicate with Todd and keep the connection between us strong.

10

FORWARD MOVEMENT

Getting myself to work in the morning after a sleepless night was daunting, but compared to the alternative it seemed the better choice. I had to get out of the house. I wondered how I would fit into the world again without my husband. I felt like an amputee. The missing parts were the best of me. I worried that those were the only parts worth anything.

Time and again, I had to force myself to remember that I was still alive, even though I felt half-dead. I had beautiful children, friends, and family who loved me, a great career, and a beautiful home. I needed to engage with life again before I fell any deeper into the despair that beckoned, especially in the middle of the night.

Keeping busy with work helped me to survive. I felt so grateful for my job. I'd always appreciated how Todd had encouraged me to fulfill my dreams of having a career even when I sometimes felt tempted to abandon them. When doubt crept in, he was always there prodding me and telling me I was strong, smart, and beautiful.

After I graduated high school, Todd had supported my desire to go to college, something no one in my immediate family had done. I was scared to be out in the world. I didn't know what I wanted to do, just that it had to be something meaningful for myself and others. It felt important that I succeed and be a source of pride to my family. I had seen a lot of pain growing up, and I wanted to help people be happy. Deep inside, I knew I could amount to something, even though my father had told me otherwise.

I registered at Rochester Community College, but I questioned my decision repeatedly. *"Who am I to have these lofty dreams?"* In the back of my mind were the reminders—my high school guidance counselor telling me I wasn't college material; my father telling me I would never amount to anything. I was scared. I wanted to go to college, but I didn't want to be away from Todd and the security I felt when I was with him. A part of me wanted nothing to change. I liked our life, even though I wanted more for us. I knew I would never forgive myself if I worked a menial job my whole life. Todd urged me to follow my dreams.

I'd felt so overwhelmed at college that I quit after the first week. I didn't know how to navigate the financial aid and scheduling and had great difficulty asking for the help I needed. Todd encouraged me to stay in school, but I dropped out and took a job at a gas station instead.

I finally went back to college in 1989 after Alexia was born. I was in my mid-twenties and determined to follow through and earn a degree this time. I graduated with an Associate's degree in business, then went on to get a Bachelor's of Science in Psychology and started working for a mental health facility. I knew a lot about mental illness from my childhood so it was a natural place for me to help others.

After Todd's death, it felt good to focus on work and the lives of the clients I served instead of my own. Over time, I slowly began to understand that Todd was not coming back. At work, I was often able to lose myself in the welcome relief of meetings, faking my way through. Tears sometimes leaked out despite my best efforts to cover my grief, but my coworkers gave me support and privacy whenever I needed them.

I was careful about who I spent my free time with, choosing to be with loved ones who really understood me, like Alexia and my sister Annette. I could be completely myself with them, and I could leave whenever I wanted to without worrying that I was hurting their feelings.

I carefully chose activities I thought I could manage. Dakota and I divided up the chores Todd used to do. I tended to the horses and yard work. Talking to the horses was great therapy. Sometimes I would sit in the barn for hours, talking and singing to them, letting the tears flow.

Work wasn't the only aspect of life that insisted on moving forward. Jackson's third birthday came just three weeks after Todd's death. Jackson had spent a lot of time with his grandpa. They'd had fun sharing popsicles, working in the garden, and reading books.

Todd and I loved to talk about the things Jackson did and his funny playful side. Todd had a small jar next to his bed that held various objects such as pennies, nuts, rocks, and bolts. Todd laughed when he showed me how Jackson liked to take the jar from the nightstand, put it on the bed, and pull out the items one by one. Then he'd put them back in the jar again with Grandpa's supervision.

In light of Todd's recent death, none of us knew how to handle Jackson's birthday. When Alexia asked me what we should do, I had no clue. The loss was still so new; we were barely getting through each day. I knew one thing: Todd would want us to celebrate.

I remember standing in Todd's shop, where we set up Jackson's party. The bar counter was full of delicious foods, and the birthday cake sat on Todd's workbench. We piled the presents next to Todd's record albums.

I watched Jackson race his Hot Wheels around the chairs, immersed in playing with his cousins and blissfully unaware of the loss the rest of us felt. I imagined Todd chasing after our grandson. He would have been in his element, talking and laughing with everyone.

A couple of weeks before Todd died, he and I had picked out a cool Radio Flyer tricycle for Jackson. Normally Todd would have been the one to put it together. But as Jackson and Dakota assembled it instead, I sensed Todd's energy in the shop. He'd loved the space, loved celebrations with family and friends. The hot burn of resentment filled me. I felt so cheated. I told myself to remember it was Jackson's day and to fake being happy, even if I felt like wailing in the corner. I couldn't help but wonder how long I'd feel so out of sorts, how long my children would wear such stunned expressions. It was heartbreaking to see their raw pain.

"Where's Grandpa?" Jackson asked several times. Alexia, Dakota, and I had done our best to explain Todd's death to Jackson in words he would understand. I hugged him and told him, "Grandpa is in heaven. We may not always see him, but he's around us and in heaven at the same time. We can talk to him, and he can hear us, even if we don't say the words aloud." I believed what I told Jackson, yet I yearned to see Todd playing with Jackson like he always had. It was such a bittersweet day.

That night after everyone left, I sat on the swing overlooking the pasture where the horses were grazing. It was a warm night. The stars were shining brightly, and frogs sang in the distance. A red-tailed hawk swooped overhead. My heart soared with it. I'd seen at least one red-tailed hawk almost every day since Todd died. Some days I'd see several of them, in flight and sitting on telephone poles. I felt sure Todd was sending them to me.

I talked to him there on the porch swing for the longest time, pouring out all my love and appreciation for him, along with my hurt and anguish about his death. I imagined him sitting right beside me like he always had and told him just how much he meant to me. I wished him well in heaven. I told him I would do my best to carry on and make him proud, like always. I vowed to get through the grief and expressed my gratitude for his beautiful soul.

It's natural to resist grief, to push it away or to ignore it. I sensed that Todd was urging me to let go of my resistance and just be with all of my feelings. I tried to allow my emotions to arise without judgment or expectation. When I did, something wonderful happened. On the other side of grief, as painful as it was, waited hope, joy and love.

A sensation of surrender washed over me. I felt Todd encouraging me to "let go." He wasn't saying, "Let *me* go." He was urging me to let go of the pain, the sadness, the disbelief, and the suffering so I could move into acceptance, peace, joy. I soon realized that allowing myself to get through my grief was a way for Todd to move forward too. We both needed each other to heal. He reminded me that we are always together, that heaven will come soon enough. Love is always and forever. It was time for me to trust that all would get better with time.

I walked up to the house feeling like I had taken another profound step toward healing. Later that night I received a text from Becky. She said, *Todd heard it all.* I knew he had; I'd felt it. Becky's confirmation solidified it. Todd's love was all around me. All my senses were heightened as gratitude for our life and our love filled me and poured out of me. Todd was telling me, "I'm here, and I will always be here for you. All the love you felt is real and always will be."

11

ALEXIA'S GIFTS

As more time passed after Todd's death, I feared I might begin to forget him in small ways, forget things he had said or done, or the feeling of him. I wanted our bond to continue to grow over time, not fray. I delved into spiritual learning with a passion born from desperation. I bought every book I could find on the subject of life after death. I sought out Becky so often I decided I needed to consult with someone else. Becky and I had become good friends, and it can be difficult to be objective when reading energy for a family member or friend.

A friend of mine knew an intuitive healer named Jenny. When I met with her, I was delighted that she connected to Todd's energy and picked up on his sense of humor right away. She told me, "Todd is bringing you the magic; he is always with you. He is one of your guides now, and he's doing his part on his side to direct you." I continued to meet with her, and she always ended the sessions by telling me Todd loves me. The more she told me this, the more I started to sense him around me. I soon learned I wasn't the only one growing more sensitive to Todd's presence.

One day Alexia brought Jackson over for a visit. I sat with her in the kitchen while Jackson played with Dakota in the living room. Alexia leaned in close to me and said, "I've been hearing Dad a lot lately."

"I imagine what he would be saying too," I told her. "I don't want to forget the sound of his voice."

A funny look crossed Alexia's face, like she wasn't sure how I'd take what she was going to say next. "I mean I'm actually talking to him in my head...and he responds. I can communicate with him, Mom."

I was elated. "What?! You can hear him? That's amazing, Alexia. Really?" I exclaimed. She looked down at the ground like she was embarrassed or uncertain and nodded her head yes.

Alexia had been honing her spiritual gifts, just like Todd had said she would when Becky spoke with him a few days after the accident. Alexia missed her conversations with her dad. They used to talk about everything. Most of the time, I would end up leaving the room before those two were finished talking. In fact, even when he was disciplining her, he would talk to her for hours. Most of the time, the discipline speeches focused on respect and being grateful for what we have. Alexia and Dakota would have gladly taken any other punishment than the hours of talking. Now, she would give anything for one more of her dad's speeches. She hadn't been as open about her grief as I had been. I tried to coax it out of her the only way I knew how, by asking her to communicate with Todd for me.

"Tell me what Dad is saying Lex; tell me what he's doing right now," I said. I worried that I was pushing her, but I wanted her to express her feelings. I knew it was hard for her and for Dakota. Their father had been such a calm, encouraging force in their life. I couldn't possibly be who he was for them. All I could do was be myself. Compared to what they had in their father, it didn't seem like it would ever be enough.

Since Todd's death, it has given me great comfort to communicate with him through Becky and Jenny. Todd was guiding me through my grief. I envied Becky and Jenny's ability to connect with him.

Becky had told me that someday I would be able to communicate with Todd like she did, and I hoped that was true despite my doubts. I wanted so badly to speak directly to my husband. That hadn't happened yet, but here was Alexia telling me she was communicating with her dad. I was brimming with excitement. Now I had another connection to Todd through our daughter. I asked her to sit in my bedroom with me so we could talk in private.

"What does he say?" I asked, once we settled in on my bed.

"Mostly he says he loves us all and that he's doing well. He says he's always with us."

"How do you know it's Dad and not your imagination?" I wanted so badly to believe her, but I couldn't help feeling that it was wishful thinking.

Alexia made a face. "Mom, I talk to him and hear his voice responding. I know it's him. I just know. I could never make this up."

I could see that she meant it. She truly believed she talked to Todd. I thought for a moment. "Can you ask him questions for me?"

Alexia frowned. "I don't know. Let's try."

"Ask him what he's doing right now." I couldn't keep the urgency and anticipation out of my tone.

There were a few moments of silence, as if Alexia was listening to someone I couldn't hear. "He's with us, and he's there at the same time," she explained. Her eyes lit with comprehension. "He can be both places simultaneously. He can be anywhere he wants, all at once."

After another long pause she said, "In heaven, there's no concept of time and space as we know it, so he can be any place just by wanting to be there. He spends time with family there and family here. He also spends time outdoors doing the things he loves."

Alexia grinned, the first genuine smile I'd seen on her face since her father died. "Mom, Dad loves you so much!"

I was overjoyed. I no longer doubted that Todd was speaking to Alexia. Becky had told me that Alexia would learn lessons from Todd's death. I felt so proud of Alexia for accepting this gift from her dad.

Jackson popped his cute little head in through the doorway. "Grandma, let's play," he said. So I started up a game of hide-and-seek. We played until it was time for Alexia and Jackson to leave. I walked them out to the car and helped Jackson get settled into the backseat, complete with a snack and extra kisses.

When I went to the driver's side to give Alexia a kiss and a hug, she gave me one last gift. "Dad says you can talk to him any time you want to. Just talk to him in your head and imagine what he would say back to you. Trust yourself."

I told her I would try, but when I didn't succeed at first, I became a little obsessed with my daughter's new abilities. I frequently asked her to tell me what her father was doing and for messages from my angels and guides. She relayed these to me orally and in letters she wrote channeling what those on the other side dictated.

At first, it was hard for her to accept that she was hearing Spirit. I was more than a little envious. I wished I could talk directly to Todd and my angels. If a close friend lost a loved one, I'd ask Alexia to connect with the deceased family member. Everything Alexia received from the other side was easily verified by the living. It helped her believe that what she was hearing was true. However, she wasn't as excited as I was. She was reluctant about her abilities. They scared her.

I kept encouraging her and reminding her that most people would love to have that connection. She didn't feel comfortable with this new "super power" and doubted herself. Over time she grew more accepting of these gifts. Her doubt lessened as the things she saw were confirmed by me and others.

12

GRIEF IS PERSONAL

Author Jamie Anderson writes, "Grief, I've learned, is really just love. It's all the love you want to give, but cannot. All of that unspent love gathers up in the corners of your eyes, the lump in your throat, and in that hollow part of your chest. Grief is just the love with no place to go."

Grief comes not only from missing our loved ones when they die but also missing the life we would have had with them. I missed looking forward to Todd coming in the front door and saying, "Hey, babe, I'm home." I miss him calling me on his work breaks just because he wants to hear my voice. Yes, grief is not only a journey, but a lesson about love. We miss them greatly, because we loved them greatly.

Elisabeth Kubler-Ross, a Swiss-American psychologist, developed the theory of the five stages of grief: Denial, Anger, Bargaining, Depression, and Acceptance. These stages have no real order to them. Sometimes these stages blend together, or they may happen all at once. However we progress through them, and in them, is natural. But, we must go through the harder stages of grief to reach acceptance. Just like other challenges in life, if we skip over them or refuse to deal with them, they will most likely come up at a later time.

For the longest time after Todd's death, my grief was wild and unpredictable. Sometimes I wrestled with it, trying not to let it take me over. Other times I was able to embrace it the way I had the night I talked to Todd under the stars. I was often surprised at the amount and the intensity of the pain and the sadness, and of the joy. My body physically ached.

My mind irrationally tried to bargain with God. Like when my mind wanted to believe that if I kept Todd's belongings, like the work pants on the end of the bed, then Todd could return and claim his physicality in our world. Denial and bargaining thoughts ran wild in my mind, creating my own alternate reality, as if I could undo what had been done.

Grief is different for each of us. It's personal. I took solace in staying busy. I let my feelings out in a trickle so they didn't devour me. That way I could still function. I wouldn't allow myself to curl up in bed for too long for fear I might never get up again. The magnitude of what had happened had to be confronted and dealt with slowly.

My grief wasn't just emotional. It was physical. Shortly after Todd died, I experienced a sudden and intense pain in my heart. It took my breath away. The pain gripped me so strongly I wondered whether I might be having a heart attack. It woke me in the middle of the night and stopped me cold throughout the day. Unlike panic attacks, which I'd had before in predictable situations, the heart pain came on at random. Sometimes the pain radiated throughout my chest and my throat. For about two years, it felt like my heart was cracking open.

No matter how hard I tried to resist them, the dark, ominous thoughts crept into my mind. *I should join Todd. I can't be here without him. What if I didn't exist anymore? I could die of a broken heart; people do that.*

A friend told me that her mother had died of a broken heart shortly after the loss of her child, my friend's brother. Doctors couldn't find any physical reason that her body gave out, but my friend and everyone close to her mom knew why. What a testament to the power of love.

I secretly yearned to be in heaven with my husband. *God*, I prayed, *let me go. Take me and my broken heart back home to Todd.* But I knew it wasn't my time to leave. My kids and my grandson needed me too much. Instead, I focused on creating as much stability and predictability for myself as possible. I went to work weekdays even if I didn't feel like it and filled my weekends with chores and family activities.

Deepak Chopra, author and alternative medicine advocate, says, "Your heart knows all the answers, so put your attention there and reflect." The heart, just like the mind and body, is resilient. And the heart, mind, and body are all connected. We all have a huge capacity to heal. But it is our choice to take the action needed to do so. We heal our hearts by emptying out the hurt that makes them ache and filling them up with love.

It seems natural that this part of the body would hurt the most, because it's the emotional storehouse, the container for all the love we feel. Living with Todd, there was so much love that my heart was overflowing. No wonder it broke wide open when he died.

Any time it seemed as if I might be swept away by my grief, I'd get a sign from Todd that helped ease me through the tumultuous emotions. Once when I was really struggling, I had an intuitive reading with a medium who immediately connected with Todd. She said he wanted me to watch for a duck formation. I told her that Todd always sent me red-tailed hawks.

She said, "This time it will be ducks."

As I was driving home from the session, a beautiful song about love and connection came on the radio. Through the tears brought on by the moving lyrics, I watched as two white ducks flew right in front of the car. They swayed in front of me for a few moments like they were dancing, moving in synchronization like ballroom dancers in the sky.

Anger is a big part of grieving, one that, in my opinion, needs to be felt and processed. Like sadness, it needs to be released from our bodies and our psyches. Taking it out on others or abusing oneself isn't healthy, but creating some private time to scream or cuss, or even to beat a pillow or break something can be cathartic.

From a very young age, I believed that it was *not* okay to be angry. I didn't even feel it was okay to voice my opinions. Throughout much of my early life I held upsetting emotions inside. I didn't know how to express my anger productively. My father had yelled and screamed at my mom and us kids. He would clench his teeth and shake his fist. My father's aggression taught me how hurtful anger can be when it is directed toward others, and I didn't want to be like him.

But anger arises for a reason. When something is wrong, it has to be acknowledged, processed, and released. I held in my rage over Todd's death for quite a while. I was afraid to feel those intense feelings, afraid of exploding. I don't think anyone has ever actually exploded from too much anger, but to me, it felt possible.

Four months after Todd's death, just before the holidays, I went to a continuing education conference on mental illness. At one point, we broke into small groups for discussion time. There were five other people in similar professions at my table.

The facilitator addressed us. "What would you do if suddenly and unexpectedly you lost the one person you love the most?" he asked. "That is how someone with major depression feels."

I thought to myself, *Really?* I looked around at my tablemates as I listened to their comments. Fury rose in me. *I DON'T HAVE TO IMAGINE,* I wanted to scream, *BECAUSE IT HAPPENED TO ME. IT'S HAPPENING RIGHT NOW.*

My ire at the conference was the first time I allowed myself to acknowledge how mad I was about Todd's death. When I finally let myself feel my anger, I raged. There were times I was so angry that I just had to be alone and wail. I'd wake up and see Todd's work pants still draped on the bed frame, or I'd go into the bathroom and open his deodorant and smell it. I wanted him back and was furious when I couldn't make that happen.

Driving to or from work, I'd listen to music at top volume. The songs evoked strong feelings. I'd start out singing at the top of my lungs until I had to pull the car over and scream and hit the steering wheel with my fists. Or I'd go into the barn or Todd's shop and yell and throw things. It felt right to scream my fury out in a private way with myself, Todd, and God; so that's what I did.

Most of my rage centered on the unfairness of it all, the self-pity I harbored. I felt that I had already been through enough with my challenging childhood and raising a son who suffered from a debilitating chronic illness. Now God had taken Todd away. It wasn't fair.

There was no way to get through my grief other than to feel my emotions—all of them. I had to give myself permission to mourn and to release the pain stuck in my body and my soul. It's okay to let the anger out and best if it's not directed toward others in damaging ways.

All I could do was focus on going through the grief and finding ways to connect with Todd. Through my spiritual studies, I've learned that human beings are made of energy. All the things we feel and the emotions we sense from others can get stuck within our energy bodies. We need to regularly clear out negative energy to keep us in an optimal state of well-being.

There are many different modes for clearing and healing. Hypnosis, meditation, visualization, and other tools can help us move through grief by giving us access to our unconscious mind and the part of us that knows everything. Some call it the Higher Self. When we're in these heightened states of awareness, we can do amazing things, including communicate with loved ones on the other side, our spirit guides, angels, and celestial beings.

Writing letters and journaling was a way for me to communicate with Todd about not only the significant things that happened, but also the mundane events of daily life. I felt a sense of deep connection with my husband through these letters.

As I wrote them, I imagined how he would respond to the events I was describing, as if he was still physically with me. It was a powerful method for keeping the connection between us strong. That connection was growing more and more every day.

Here is a letter I wrote to Todd about a year-and-a-half after he died.

December, 2014
Dearest Todd,

Miss you, babe! I was just thinking about the word "raw." You used to use it in such a playful way, and now it describes this deep hurt I feel, a hurt that has lessened in intensity but still ambushes me from time to time.

Do you like it there? I feel you everywhere.

I'm going to Maui with Alexia next month. You'll be there, too, I know it.

I had Jackson over Friday night. He still kisses your picture and has me kiss it, too. He says you're in the clouds.

I often think about what we would be doing had you stayed here. The conversations we'd have, playing with Jackson, the smiles, the laughter, and the struggles. I miss it all. In a few more years, I'll be older than you. That's hard. It's so good to write to you, but so hard to do.

Someday while I'm still alive, I'm going to visit you in heaven. It will be wonderful, vivid, and amazing. I can't wait. I also can't wait to join you when it's my time. But right now the kids need me. I have things to do, don't I? Thanks for your help. I always knew you loved me. Now I know the depth of your love—expansive, unconditional, beautiful, amazing love.

Xoxo,
You're the best, and the love of my life.
Brenda

A few years later, right around Todd's birthday, I got a tattoo as a tribute to his love. I chose feathers symbolizing red-tailed hawks; a daisy surrounded by an infinity sign; Todd's words, "love forever," from a letter he'd once written me; and an "O-X" from a more recent letter he wrote me. (Todd always wrote "oxox" on cards and letters, instead of "xoxo" like most people do.) Many people get tattoos in honor of loved ones. It's another of the many ways we can feel connected.

The grieving process is so unique and personal, but one thing about it is universal. Everyone struggles when they lose a loved one, and everyone needs support; maybe not right away, but at some point in the process. I never knew what to do or what to say when I met someone who was grieving. Now it was my turn to experience that awkwardness from others. I treasured even the smallest offerings, every act of kindness, from cleaning the house to bringing necessities to going out for coffee or lunch.

I was grateful for the love that surrounded me after Todd died. I thought a lot about the things family and friends said to me at the funeral. Todd's nieces had mentioned how he always said, "Isn't it a beautiful day?"

His friends had marveled at his contagious laugh and his ability to live in the present and love life. Todd had a habit of telling funny stories with so many details and expressions that even his friends had to be wishing he'd get to the point already. He would usually end a story by laughing at himself with deep satisfied belly laughs. I found myself smiling through my tears as I savored those memories.

I didn't want to forget anything.

No one could bring Todd back, but the kindness of my friends and loved ones helped me to heal. So many people offered their help. Even though I wouldn't always take them up on the help, I appreciated the offers more than I can express.

My lovely coworkers sent me a garden arrangement with a green bulb extending out into the air. Vicki painted the word "Breathe" on the bulb, along with a white daisy. Every time I passed by it, I took a deep breath. Several friends reminded me about the things I needed to do to maintain the house, like changing the HVAC filters and replacing the salt for the water softener. Family and friends helped fix things, and Todd's friend Craig brought over hay for the horses. Other friends created a phone list and said I had permission to call them at any hour.

I tried to remind myself frequently of what I felt grateful for, especially the people in my life. Shannon, Todd's best friend from high school, told me, "Isn't it great that you have Dakota living with you, so you're not alone?" He was right; having Dakota at home was a blessing. I also had Alexia, her partner Troy, and my grandson just twenty minutes away. Todd's sister Lynn and her husband, Tim, lived right next door, and my neighbor and dear friend Vicki was a mile away.

Todd knew how to feel joy. He also knew how to process sadness, anger, and fear and return to a state of well-being. That's what I strive to do now—allow myself to feel what I feel, whether it's happiness or grief. Healing can take time.

Eventually, the memories will only feel good, with no lingering sadness or grief. Thinking about all the beautiful memories of my time with Todd is so much more than just remembering. It's another way to connect to him on a deeper level. Recalling a memory is essentially like reliving it with our loved ones. Remembering bridges the distance between us.

I still often daydream about things Todd would say if he was with me now. If I meditate on it long enough, it feels like it's actually happening in the present moment. It's another way for me to keep our love alive, one that has brought me tremendous comfort over the years.

13

A YEAR OF FIRSTS

The year following Todd's death was full of firsts. The first Christmas, our wedding anniversary, and all the birthdays, including his in October, just three months after he passed away. Todd had always enjoyed celebrating his birthday. The kids and I loved how expressive he was when opening his gifts. "Thank you so much, I love this!" he'd exclaim. If he got clothes he would put them on over the ones he was wearing. He'd put a whole pack of socks on, one over another until he couldn't fit any more.

Todd had turned fifty years old just nine months before he passed. I'd wanted to surprise him with something he would remember for years. We usually had a party on his birthday since he loved to celebrate, but that year it needed to be something really special. I thought hard about what would be best—a fancy trip, maybe, or renting a hot rod. I finally decided to ask Todd what he'd like. I told him to think big.

He said sheepishly, "It would be fun to have a band play." He was enjoying the band at the barbeque festival in Faribault where we were hanging out with my nephew and his wife. When the Rusty Nails took a break, I snuck away to ask the guitar player about booking a private party.

After a few phone calls with the band leader, I told Todd we were going to have a barn dance for his birthday. There was no way I could surprise him; it would take a lot of work to get the barn ready. We had to rearrange the horse tack, pressure wash the cobwebs from the walls, string lights, and decorate. Todd's sister Lynn and my sister Annette and the kids helped us get the barn ready. Alexia made a huge banner with five decades' worth of photos of Todd. He couldn't wait to have the party.

I remember Todd asking me a few days before if I'd like to dance at the party. I seldom danced at family functions, but Todd loved to dance. I'd seen the disappointed look on his face so many times throughout the years when he would ask me to dance and I turned him down. So that time I told him, "It's your day. If you want me to dance, I'll dance the whole night with you."

The night of the party, as soon as the music started, Todd stopped what he was doing and came running around the corner into the barn. I was sitting with a couple of my friends on a hay bale, watching the band, when he grabbed my arm and swung me onto the dance floor. I'll never forget the look of pure joy in his eyes. We danced a lot that night. So many of his friends and family had come to celebrate with us. Todd couldn't stop talking about how even some of his high school classmates had shown up.

I would give anything for one more dance with Todd. Whenever I'm given the opportunity to dance now, I take it. Todd taught me how important it is to enjoy every moment.

I wasn't sure how to spend Todd's birthday that first year after he died. I knew I wanted to be with the kids, and Todd had always loved Red Lobster, so I took Alexia, Dakota and Jackson there for dinner. Alexia ordered the dish Todd always got, Walt's Favorite Shrimp.

I told the waitress we were celebrating a special birthday for someone who wasn't with us, but I knew Todd was there. I asked for a cupcake with a candle on it. I thought singing to him would lighten the mood and honor Todd's special day. The waitress brought the cupcake and lit the candle. She lowered her head and said she was sorry as she slid the cupcake toward the middle of the table. The candle went out. The kids and I just looked at each other and chose not to sing.

The kids and I decided that we would continue to celebrate Todd's birthday together every year, but not do anything celebratory on the anniversary of his death once we got through the first one. Dakota was adamant: Todd's birthday was the day to celebrate.

After we returned home from dinner that evening, I laid down on the bed and imagined the way we would have celebrated if Todd was still alive. I told him I would have gotten him a matching cabinet to go with his tool bench, and he would have stayed up late putting it together. I imagined enjoying watching him work on it, like I always did. There's something so sexy about watching a man working. I sensed Todd encouraging me to savor my memories and my imaginings. He urged me to do whatever I could to feel something other than the grief that weighed me down, to find a sense of delight instead.

Todd had to remind me to include the importance of a sense of humor in this book. A sense of humor can be a soothing balm throughout all of the stages of grief. Humor is contagious, beautiful, and healing. It helps us soften the pain and let our worries go. As we move through the healing process, we shouldn't be afraid to laugh and enjoy life.

There was a time when I thought I would never laugh again. Todd helped me see that our lives are not supposed to stop, even when we are grieving a profound loss. We are not meant to suffer. It's okay to laugh. It's okay to feel joy. It doesn't mean we love our loved ones any less. While we may feel guilty about experiencing happiness after someone we love dies, feeling better emotionally doesn't mean we don't love and want our loved ones back. It means we care about ourselves and enjoying the life we have.

Todd often tells me from the other side to lighten up. He wants me to enjoy life the best I can at every moment. He brought so much humor into our lives, and he doesn't want the laughter to stop. He loved to laugh and have a good time and always told me not to be so serious. He had a deep Ed McMahon-style laugh, the kind that went on and on. He'd laugh at anything funny, including himself. I've never known anyone to laugh at themselves the way he did. He saw the humor in the big things and the small things. His energy filled a room and lit up everyone in it. I loved watching him when he was with his friends. His body shaking with laughter, he'd hold his stomach and complain that it hurt from so much laughing.

Dakota and Alexia talked about the way Todd and I used to laugh as they were growing up. Alexia said to Dakota, "Remember how mom and dad used to laugh upstairs in their bedroom?"

Dakota said, "Yeah, it went on for hours."

"Oh dear," I said. "We tried to keep it down."

Alexia said, "No, we both loved it, mom."

I told them I remembered us both laughing so much my stomach hurt, trying to be quiet so we wouldn't wake them. Old houses have thin walls.

Since Todd died, I've developed a deep laugh that is different from my usual higher-pitched laugh. Dakota and I chuckle at how much my new laugh sounds like Ed McMahon's.

14

THE ROAD TO REMEMBRANCE

I felt immense relief when the first anniversary of Todd's death arrived. The entire year had been like peeling the scab off a wound as we struggled through all of the firsts without Todd— the holidays, birthdays, and special occasions. To get through the anniversary of his death, Alexia, Dakota, and I took a road trip to South Dakota to see Shannon, Todd's best friend from high school.

The day Todd died, Dakota had called Shannon, who'd jumped into his pickup truck and made the ten-hour drive to our house. After the funeral, Shannon took a rose quartz rock from South Dakota out of the back of his pickup and placed it near Todd's shop. As Dakota and I admired the beautiful stone, Shannon said, "Now all we need is time."

A year later, in some ways it felt like no time had passed, while in other ways, it felt like an eternity. Regardless, Shannon's words were comforting and hopeful. As we passed landmarks along the way, the kids reminisced about previous road trips they'd taken with their dad to visit Shannon over the years. Here is one story Alexia told me about her memories from South Dakota. I had her write it down for me so I wouldn't forget.

I have fond memories of going to SD with Dad and Dakota. Summer of 2010 was our last trip together. We were at the cabin. We woke up, ate breakfast on the porch and walked outside to be near the wildlife. Dad loved being in nature. We ended up going to the border of the Black Hills National Forest. It was truly breathtaking and surreal. We stopped at a huge rock and sat on the ledge to take a picture. Dad always counted on me to take the family photos. I would sometimes sigh, like it was a burden, but I loved that he depended on me for that.

On the walk, we came across cattle, eagles, and hawks. We discovered so much right before us, things we would normally miss in our everyday lives. I loved how Dad's eyes lit up when he talked about the animals, especially the birds. We discovered a cave near the end of our walk. It was just pure happiness and fun between us. I'll never forget how in sync we felt and how we were caught up in living in the moment (like dad always instructed us to do). I had my fancy camera you and dad bought for me, and I took pictures like crazy.

When we neared the cabin, we stopped and checked out Shannon's horse wagon. Dad said he wanted to build one, so he asked me to take some pictures for him. I had the feeling it wouldn't be long before he'd build one. Sure enough, when we got home from that trip he started making plans to build the wagon. He was so excited about building it so he could hitch up the horses and take us on family rides down the gravel roads and in the pasture.

Remember mom? The next summer Dad built the wagon. We all helped. I brought him water and peanut butter sandwiches. He finished it late in the fall of that year. I'll always have those fond memories fresh in my mind and heart. I'm beyond proud to be his daughter.

As we drove the windy roads to South Dakota, admiring the tall trees, we put in our traditional James Taylor road trip music. It felt like Todd was with us, as the kids joked and at times, got caught up in mixed emotions as they shared their memories. Along the way, we saw a man carving statues of eagles. We stopped and asked if he could make a red-tailed hawk statue. It is now a great addition to Todd's memorial garden and a lovely reminder of our time together in South Dakota.

At the end of the trip, we spent a night at Shannon's cabin, deep in the woods near Pringle. The four of us sat on the porch before we said our goodbyes while Shannon shared memories of Todd. "Your dad was kind of crazy in high school," Shannon chuckled. The kids learned a few things that surprised them that night. We'll just leave it at that.

We marveled at the bittersweet irony that Shannon had been planning a visit later during the summer that Todd passed. Shannon had bought a motorcycle and was going to ride to Minnesota on it. He had been planning to show up and surprise Todd. I imagined Todd's face when Shannon pulled up on a motorcycle. There would have been a lot of laughing and a big hug, I'm sure. Todd couldn't wait to go on motorcycle rides. He would ride with his friend Craig and his sister Lynn and her husband, Tim, whenever he got the chance.

When it was time for us to drive back to Minnesota, I left Shannon Todd's favorite belt with his Harley Davidson belt buckle on it, along with a note thanking Shannon for his friendship. The belt buckle was one of the only things I felt compelled to part with besides Todd's motorcycle jacket, which I'd given to his sister Lynn. After hearing Shannon's plans for the surprise motorcycle trip, it was no wonder I was prompted by Todd to bring it for him. Later that day, Shannon called and told Dakota how meaningful the belt was to him.

That trip felt like a rite of passage. It brought a sense of release. I knew I'd continue to grieve Todd, but with time, the intensity would lessen. Just as Shannon had said after Todd's funeral.

Loving myself includes choosing to be happy again. Choosing happiness doesn't negate what Todd and I had while he was alive.

Love is love. Long-term unhappiness, pain, and suffering doesn't serve anyone. I've reached a deeper acceptance of my husband's death. I'm able to think about Todd with smiles again instead of tears. I love knowing that the bond we share will never be broken.

At the same time, I've had to face the fact that our relationship has changed. Both of us have grown and evolved. Thanks to Todd's unconditional love and guidance, I can actually say I like my life again. This is how it should be. Todd wants me to live fully. Holding onto the past in a way that made me sad and angry wasn't helping me move forward.

Happiness and joy are choices, and sometimes it takes strength to choose them. Sometimes it feels like the only choice is to be willing to move *toward* peace, accepting whatever emotion I feel in any given moment. I appreciate feelings of joy and happiness when they come. Todd wants all of us—his children, grandchildren, family, and friends—to live happily, with lots of love and laughter. I could lie in bed, depressed and focused on what I've lost, but that wouldn't honor the life that I have. And it wouldn't honor Todd.

Sometimes I look around and wonder where all the time has gone, but I also feel like no time has passed. I think about my new life and the direction I'm taking. I am a survivor. Todd used to tell me that all the time, but I didn't buy in. Now I can see it in myself. Todd is showing me. And he's right. I am strong. I am capable. He is telling me I will not only survive, but I will thrive again. I feel Todd prodding me along. He is always with me.

15

CHOOSING LIFE

ncouraged by Alexia's success in reaching Todd, I kept trying to talk with him myself. One day, I was walking my dog Stanley, when I heard Todd say in my mind, "Hi babe, it's me. I love you, and I'm right here with you where I'll always be."

I thought, this is nice, but it must be my imagination. I must be making this up because I want to hear him so badly. I walked back to the house and called Alexia.

"Can you talk to Dad and ask him if something is true?" I asked her. She had been in contact with Todd for a while, and I trusted what she channeled from him unreservedly.

Before I could go on she said, "Dad says he's talking to you, and YES, you are hearing him. He says not to doubt it."

Elation filled me. *I could hear Todd!* He was talking directly to me. I wouldn't have to depend on anyone else to talk with him. I jumped up and down, giddy with excitement. After that, with a little practice, I was able to hear Todd talking clearly to me. When he did, I got images of him smiling or making gestures.

Sometimes he also gave me a sign. I might see a red-tailed hawk and immediately hear him say, "I love you, babe." The more

I practiced, the easier it became. It felt a little bit like tuning the frequency knob on the radio to reach a particular station. I talked to him and then quietly listened as I imagined him answering me.

Once I strengthened my connection with Todd, my grief loosened its hold a little bit. I started to think about moving forward with my new life, and I realized that I didn't have to do it alone. Todd was still helping me.

This whole experience has taught me that I'm strong. Even though Todd would tell me this all the time, I'd always felt like he saw something in me that wasn't really there, as if I was fooling him. I surely wasn't the strong, confident, outgoing person he thought I was. But as I rose above some of the pain and grief, I saw that Todd had been right. I *was* capable. I *was* strong.

I would not only survive, but it was possible that someday I might even thrive again. Todd is guiding me, and through this journey, I can see my strength and that I have a choice in how I move through my life experiences.

The unimaginable can bring a new perspective. With Todd's death, I began to understand my own resilience. It surprised me. His death taught me that I can probably handle anything. Whenever I'm faced with something unexpected or uncomfortable, I'm less fearful now than I was before. Nothing could be worse than losing Todd, so there's no longer anything to fear. Besides, I'm learning that he is not truly lost to me.

We all have a choice about what we take from our experiences. We are all strong and powerful; we just forget sometimes. We can feel sorry for ourselves, or we can rise up and experience all the love around us. I chose to move through my grief and come out the other side. Todd is physically gone and in heaven, but I remain connected to him. I appreciate all the love and beauty that we shared and continue to share. I am writing my own story about Todd's death and how I will live on.

In "Tears to Triumph," Marianne Williamson writes, "We suffer to the extent that we identify with the brokenness of the world. Our power to heal lies in the knowing that we actually are not of this world." Here on earth, our egos keep us caught up in our human needs, worries, and concerns. When we unite with Spirit, also known as Source, God, Highest Self, and a host of other names, Spirit supports and leads in miraculous ways.

When we pay attention, we can see this guidance clearly. We remember who we really are as we align with our most powerful, divine selves. Todd was helping me to do just that, and he continues to do so now. He sees the real ME when I can't. Our loved ones do this for us all the time.

For years, I had been drawn to seeking the meaning of life through the metaphysical, the paranormal, the mystical. I had read books on spiritual subjects in my spare time, but my studies never went beyond reading until I met Becky. I learned so much from Becky's guidance and her direct communication with Spirit. She opened my eyes to the mysteries of the universe.

Now I'm starting to see just how my decisions create my life. There may be a divine plan, but we get to choose the path we take through life to get there. Most importantly, we get to decide how to perceive our experiences.

I remember so many times Todd saying to me and the kids, "Make the best of it." We have a choice in how we learn our lessons. Through my learning, I've come to realize that everything we experience leads us to where we need to be in divine timing. The best part is, we can't make a mistake. *Everything* is a lesson.

Author Tracy Farquhar writes, "Every day you are faced with choices which build the structure of your life's path, and which afford you the opportunity to create the most lucrative path for your soul's wisdom and experience." Even though we go through challenging experiences, we never have to suffer. Suffering is a choice. Nothing we say or do could ever make us unworthy of love. We are always loved and guided by an abundance of angels, guides, and loved ones.

All these things that Becky and other spiritual guides talked about resonated with the spiritual lessons I had read and brought them to life in a deeper way. My conversations with Todd confirmed much of what I had read and heard. As some of my grief subsided, it was replaced by an urge to learn more.

Todd tells me that heartbreak is an illusion. Disappointment is part of human nature, and it blocks our soul's path and our growth. We hold ourselves back with our dark fears and thoughts. In the early days after Todd died, I couldn't imagine a time I would ever feel healed enough to enjoy life again or look forward to my future. I adopted the attitude of faking it until I made it, not believing it would be possible to feel joy and love again.

As I discovered more ways to connect to Todd and feel his love, I gained peace in knowing we are never alone. Todd tells me I am whole, and he reminds me that in many ways we are more connected now than when he was alive. Now I truly know that I am never alone. Separation is an illusion. Unconditional love is the only true reality. There are infinite ways to connect.

16

SIGNS ARE EVERYWHERE

The winter following Todd's death was brutal. Dakota and I were still navigating how to manage the household affairs, and we were more than a little nervous about the cold weather months. We were right to worry—we had record snow accumulations that year. We had to tunnel our way out of all the snow.

As I walked out every morning to feed the horses, I thought about Todd and all the times he'd woken early or stayed out late to care for them. Minnesota winters are harsh, but Todd had a way of making me feel warm on even the chilliest of days. He thought the snow was pretty and often reminded me of its beauty. He knew how to keep our house well heated and took care of all the necessary preparations to get us through the season.

When it was really cold out, he'd start my car before work, scrape my windows, and shovel a path to the car for me. He made me feel so safe and cared for every day. I tried to never take Todd for granted, but since his death, I appreciated the little things he'd done daily even more.

For months, I had been begging Todd to visit me in physical form. I had read accounts of people seeing their deceased loved ones for a moment or two. In the book "Hello from Heaven" by Bill Guggenheim and Judy Guggenheim, people share stories about visits from deceased family and friends, where they could speak with their loved ones through telepathy, reading one another's thoughts without speaking. The deceased beings lower their energetic vibrations, and the humans raise theirs so that they can align and meet in the middle. My aunt Diane also told me about a time when her late husband visited her in the kitchen. She said it was so real that it couldn't have been her imagination.

The day of the first big snowfall, I was shoveling off the patios, cussing as I tossed large chunks of snow onto the grass by the garage. Out of the corner of my eye, I caught a glimpse of Todd on the cement landing I had just shoveled off. He was wearing his work clothes. I stopped, stunned. Just as quickly as he'd appeared, he faded away again.

Todd hadn't said anything, but I knew he'd come to give me an important message. He wished he could be there to shovel the snow for me, to start my car, to take away the harshness of the winter, the way he had always done before. He was telling me that even though he couldn't be there in person, he was with me in spirit.

Todd sends me signs of his presence all the time. In addition to the red-tailed hawks I've seen almost daily since he died, he's found other ways to show me he's watching over us. When I was at the nursery purchasing the maple tree for Todd's memorial garden, I shared the tree's significance with the nursery owner. He led me over to a miniature conifer.

"This is called a Tree of Life," he said. "I want you to have it for your garden."

I looked long and hard for the right spot for the special Tree of Life. I thought I'd found it, but I hit a root and was unable to plant it there. I started to dig in a couple of other places, but they didn't seem right either. Then I dug a small hole near the red shed. At the bottom of the hole was a nail. I'd been finding nails lying around all over the place for a while. Becky had said they were signs from Todd, so I'd been saving them in a glass jar. The one in the hole was confirmation of the right spot to plant the tree.

Once when I returned from a trip, Alexia handed me a folded piece of paper. "I found a note from Dad tucked in the sleeve of a notebook," she said.

It was a handwritten note that read, "Brenda, just remember, that ain't all you got!" A big smiley face was drawn in the center of the paper. "We love you and miss you. Have a blast! And call us. Love forever, Todd."

Todd must have tucked it in my suitcase before I went on some trip. It was the perfect sign after coming home and wishing I could land in his arms.

A couple of years after Todd died, I went on a cruise with my friend Michelle. We stayed in Savannah, Georgia, for a couple of days before the cruise; I instantly fell in love with the city. As we walked around the beautiful neighborhoods, Michelle suggested we do karaoke that night. Neither one of us had done it before. What better way to do karaoke for the first time than in a strange town where no one knew us?

I decided I'd sing "Yellow" by Coldplay. I love the hopeful message of the song and thought it would be nice to sing to Todd. We practiced our songs all day as we took in the sights of Savannah. When we got to a karaoke bar that night, they had every Coldplay song available except Yellow. I was so bummed, I bowed out altogether.

When we later arrived at the cruise ship, we walked into the piano bar. The first song the piano player chose was "Yellow." Michelle and I sang at the top of our lungs. Todd was definitely sending me a message, letting me know he was there with us. My interpretation from him was that life can be all yellow—sunshine and bliss—if I allow it.

On the last day of our trip, I wandered into a shop at the airport. A decorative sign read, "Rise and Shine." I thought it was beautiful, but I had already spent a lot of money, so I didn't purchase it. I regretted my decision as soon as we boarded the plane, but by then, it was too late.

I said to Michelle, "I should have bought that sign. It was all yellow." Suddenly it hit me: not only was that a line from the Coldplay song, but the sign was painted yellow! Another clever sign from Todd. Michelle and I laughed and cried so hard we annoyed the other passengers, but I didn't care. The signs were so clear, and my emotions were so full. I called the airport store and purchased the sign as soon as I got home. I put it in my bedroom as a reminder to face each day with anticipation and excitement.

Todd isn't the only one who sends me signs from the other side. During a really tough time in the autumn of 2014, Dakota was in and out of the hospital for several months with complications from cystic fibrosis. On the way up to his hospital room one day, I stopped in the gift shop. There was a beautiful angel statue inscribed with the words, "Peace be with you."

My mom always used to say, "Peace be with you." Her mission was to spread that message to people everywhere she went, whether they wanted to hear it or not. I took the statue as a much-needed and appreciated sign from my mom.

Another time I was sitting in my living room watching "Eat, Pray, Love," a movie about a woman on a pilgrimage to Italy, India, and Bali, who learns to live in the moment and enjoy life's pleasures. When I walked downstairs to let my dogs outside during a commercial break, my eyes immediately went to the memoir by the same title, which was sitting on the shelf that lined my basement steps. I opened the book, and out fell my mother's obituary.

Her beautiful face gazed up at me. It was as if she was reaching out to tell me, "Don't forget, I'm here and I love you, Brenda."

Despite her tragic mental illness, my mother was highly creative and very affectionate. It was so perfect that I had put her obituary in "Eat, Pray, Love."

One day, Alexia told me that my mom wanted me to know that she sings me a song every day. Mom was a beautiful singer. She loved to talk with Jesus and often wrote spiritual songs. She had several songs that she sang whenever we were together.

"Which one does she sing?" I asked Alexia.

"She doesn't want me to tell you. She says you'll know." Alexia told me to wake up the next day and listen for Mom singing to me.

The next morning, I tried to tune into Mom's spirit. To my surprise, I heard her loud and clear, singing, "Hallelujah, He is mine, precious Lord divine. He will live with us forever. Forever, forever, he will live with us forever." I heard it so clearly that it jolted me out of bed.

Mom said, "Can you hear me Brenda? I'm here with you."

I couldn't wait to tell Alexia what had happened. Alexia told me that Mom has a different song for each of us. She chose to sing "Hallelujah" to me because that song reflected how she felt about being my mother.

Little children are often so connected to Spirit that they don't perceive any separation from it. They receive signs all the time. Wouldn't it be nice if it could be like that for all of us, all the time?

One afternoon, when Jackson was about four years old, we were in the kitchen having a snack when he told me that Todd visited him in dreams.

"Grandpa comes in real life, too," he went on. His eyes got huge. "It's for *real*, Grandma."

I had to chuckle.

Then he said, "Grandpa teleports."

That got my attention. I set down my tea mug. "What do you mean?" I asked.

"Grandpa sends parts of himself to be with ALL of us. He's with me and Mom at the same time."

I thought about this for a moment. "And he's with me and Dakota too?"

Jackson grinned, happy that I understood. "Yes, all of us! He kisses you every night, Grandma. When Grandpa leaves he says, 'Goodbye, I love you, I love you the most.'" He told me again that Todd kisses me goodnight every night and that he sees Grandpa all the time.

Todd's presence continues to impact Jackson in positive ways. Alexia, Dakota and I try hard to keep Todd alive in Jackson by talking about Todd often and encouraging Jackson to tell us when he feels Todd is with him.

I've talked to many people about the importance of signs from our loved ones. These signs are reminders of just how often our loved ones are thinking of us. The love they hold for us is immense. While we may not be able to see them in physical form, they remain with us forever.

17

GOING WITHIN

Some time after Todd passed, I was talking to my coworker Joy. "Joy, I think I want to take some courses and learn how to do hypnosis," I confided. "I've been looking into some classes."

Joy looked at me kind of funny and said, "Brenda, you've only been talking about wanting to learn hypnosis ever since I met you."

"I have?" I said.

She laughed. "Yes, Brenda, you have."

Joy was right. I *had* talked about it off and on for years but could never justify spending money on taking courses. I don't know why I hadn't pursued it. Todd would have supported anything I felt passionate about.

My fascination with hypnosis started in high school. Brian, a friend of my brother Adrian, and I had gotten into a lengthy discussion about spirituality one night. Brian claimed that anyone could be hypnotized and remember their past and even relive it. In fact, he said that not only could you go back and remember your childhood, it was also possible to go back in time and remember *past lives*. This was the first time I was introduced to the concept. I was fascinated.

Brian explained that many of our souls have been here on earth for hundreds, even thousands, of lifetimes. He said he thought I was an "old soul" and that I'd lived many lives on earth. He explained, "We continue to come back to learn so our souls can experience what it means to be human."

The more Brian talked, the more I wanted to know. So much about life felt ordinary and mundane, but these mysterious subjects lit me up with excitement and awe. We talked the entire evening and into the early morning hours. I'll never forget our discussion and the imprint it left on me.

A few weeks after my chat with Joy, I had a session with Becky. "Todd is saying that you should learn hypnosis," she said. "It's something you've always wanted to do, so go for it."

I was stunned. I'd never told Becky that I was interested in hypnosis. I took her message as a sign from Todd and registered for a course in the Twin Cities, about an hour's drive from my home. I sat down in the small classroom with three other women, sensing instinctively that I was in the right place at the right time.

The instructor, Devin Hastings, gave everyone in class a hug, and I could tell immediately that it was going to be a great experience. He explained that hypnosis was really self-hypnosis, and that it was based in self-love. Not only would we learn how to guide someone into hypnosis, we would also receive healing through the course as Devin demonstrated hypnosis on us.

On the second day of class, Devin led us in our first hypnosis session. Everyone settled in, with some resting their heads against the back wall and putting their feet up on chairs. Others took off their shoes. I observed and followed their lead.

Devin said, "Close your eyes."

I followed his voice, found myself distracted, and then listened again. A part of me was doubtful anything would happen. As my body relaxed, pictures formed in my mind. I envisioned myself on the front steps of my home. For months, every time I'd passed by the door dividing the kitchen and living room from the bedrooms, I'd experienced a sudden sharp sensation of losing my feet from underneath me. That was where I'd been standing the moment everything changed when the officer told me about Todd's accident. I had walked past that spot hundreds of times since. Every time, I'd been gripped by that terrible pain.

Suddenly, *there he was.*

Todd was standing on the steps in his work jeans, a white button-down shirt, and bare feet. His hair was shoulder-length like it had been for many years before he shaved it off. He looked so good. He was smiling and gently holding my hand. His hazel eyes glistened in the sunlight. He didn't speak a word, but I could sense him telling me, "I'm here, babe. I was on that day, too."

He was talking about the day the sheriff and the chaplain came to give me the news about the accident. Tears streamed down my face. Todd had chosen the steps to meet me with a message: *I am going to replace this memory, lighten it up for you so that when you think of the steps to our beautiful home, you can see me here holding your hand instead of that painful time. I am always here. See us together, holding hands on the steps. Think about our love, our family, our happy life together, and know I'm here with you every step of the way.*

I opened my eyes and found myself back in the classroom. Everyone around me still had their eyes closed. Devin smiled warmly at me. I closed my eyes again and returned to the steps. Todd sat with me and we looked at the sky together, enjoying the beautiful sunny day until the sounds in the classroom grew louder and Devin ended the session. I cried, and Devin said the sweetest thing. "Let the tears come. They're liquid gold, and it's beautiful," he said. I told everyone what I'd seen and felt, and each person in class hugged me. I had connected with Todd in yet another way.

As the rest of my fellow students took a break and stepped outside for some fresh air, I thought back to the meeting with Becky in the basement a few days after Todd died. Todd had been sitting on the basement steps talking through Becky to us, telling us that just like in the Aerosmith song, he didn't want to miss a thing.

I was grateful for the encounter I'd just had with Todd. It was not the same as having him with me physically, but it felt like the next best thing. It was clear to me that it was time to take more steps forward on my journey. But I didn't have to do it alone. I promised him that with him by my side I would take the necessary steps.

One of the most profound lessons I gleaned from Devin's hypnosis course was that it's not what happens to us that matters, it's the stories *about* what happened that create a significant impact. In other words, it's all in our perspective—how we think and feel about what happens to us.

I took several courses with Devin, working my way up to the master hypnosis course. Whenever we meditate, go inside and turn to our divine selves, we can love and heal ourselves in profound ways. The following story demonstrates just how powerful the mind and body connection is and how healing can occur.

I went out early one morning to throw hay to the horses and discovered Carmel lying on the ground in a pool of blood. She was slumped over, breathing laboriously. From the amount of blood around her it looked like she had been lying there a long time. I couldn't tell where she was hurt. I had to act fast. I ran to Dakota's room in the basement, frantically yelling for him. My whole body shook as I imagined the worst. Carmel would likely die. I could hardly catch my breath as I directed Dakota to call the vet, while I used my phone to call my neighbor Vicki.

It took the vet forty-five minutes to get to our house. Meanwhile, Vicki and her daughter Ellie arrived. Dakota and Ellie found some horse supplies, and all of us tried to calm Carmel and temporarily stop the bleeding until the vet arrived. Carmel had cut her leg deeply, apparently kicking the tin on the side of the barn. It dawned on me that she and Abby, our pony, must have been picking through the manure pile near the barn to get at hay.

Thankfully, the vet said she would be fine, and after several weeks, Carmel was healing from her injury. We'd gotten really lucky. But it was a huge ordeal. The horse lost a lot of blood. If I hadn't gotten there when I did, she wouldn't have made it. For several days after the accident, I panicked and shook every time I walked out to the barn to care for the horses. I was experiencing PTSD symptoms from the traumatic event.

When I told Devin about Carmel's accident, he asked me to close my eyes. He guided me through replaying the events of walking to the barn and discovering Carmel in a pool of blood. He had me view it as a movie playing out scene by scene. At times, he slowed down or sped up the scene and changed it from color to black and white. He ended the session when I was able to walk through the events without feeling any panic or anxiety.

When I woke the next day, I thought for a second about Carmel and got a slight feeling of discontent but was able to walk to the barn and care for the horses without the strong reaction. I had no panic or shaking walking to the barn to feed the horses. Carmel was healing, and I was too. I believe the PTSD symptoms would have continued had I not been guided to change it.

Once I learned hypnosis, I did practice sessions with Alexia. After a little convincing, she was willing to give it a try. She was surprised to discover how easily she could get into a hypnotic state and fully immerse herself into the garden I suggested she step into. She completely trusted the process and let go of any disbelief so that she could be fully present.

In our sessions, Alexia always met her dad in the same garden. She told me she physically felt like she was there with Todd. Tears rolled down her cheeks when she described the sense of peace and love she felt visiting with her father there. One time she told me she'd seen Todd and all our loved ones who had passed, along with our pets that had also died. They were all together underneath Todd's maple tree in the memorial garden we'd planted in his honor. Alexia said everyone's energies blended together, showing her that we are all connected.

Another time, Alexia asked me to write down some questions for Todd. I debated about asking a particular question. Part of me wanted to know what Todd and I would be doing together if he hadn't passed. Another part wasn't sure I could bear to hear the answer. Finally, I decided to ask about it.

Alexia grew emotional. "Dad is still working at Crown Cork and Seal. The two of you are looking forward to the summer and doing some fun things together since you've been working so hard on landscaping projects. You've even put in a pond."

My heart sank. I knew that was exactly what we would be doing. The summer after we'd bought the house we had worked hard on the yard.

After my conversation with Alexia, I looked at the sketches of the backyard that Todd had drawn before he died. Sure enough, there was a pond. It was part of Todd's plan.

It's hard not to miss that life. A part of me will always want that and only that. The angels tell me to appreciate what I have and not to focus on what could have been. They encourage me to move forward and appreciate the beauty and love all around me. That's what I strive to do.

After several sessions, I asked Alexia, "Could you allow Dad to talk to me through you while your consciousness sits in the garden?" I'd heard of others who were able to channel beings on the other side, and hoped that Alexia could do it too, but I wasn't sure whether anything would happen.

She was willing to try. I guided my daughter into the garden. She immediately connected to her animals and imagined the garden like she always did, making it her own sanctuary. I directed her to see herself lying on a blanket in the garden. When she was relaxed, I asked her to allow Todd to speak directly to me through her.

A few moments later, Alexia opened her eyes and said, "Hi, sweetie." Her hands stretched out toward mine like Todd's always had. "I love you." The tone was deeper than my daughter's, and the words came out more slowly than Alexia's usual quick speech.

It was Todd.

I cried as he spoke of the future and how everything would work out. This might sound impossible, but it happened. Todd and I connected through Alexia. She channeled his spirit. The experience was beyond beautiful. I was finally having a direct conversation with Todd. I didn't ever want it to end.

I asked Todd what he did in heaven.

"A lot of the same things I did when I was there," he said. "I'm teaching others how to build things from wood." Just before he died, Todd had been building some beautiful wooden benches out of a dead tree on our property. He'd planned to make one for everyone in the family.

Todd said that in heaven, people learn certain skills. They bring along those skills when they're born again into new lives. He also spent time with his loved ones who were deceased, and he was watching over all of us on earth. He could be everywhere he wanted to be at once.

"I'm also helping others connect to their loved ones through out-of-body experiences," he added.

We chuckled about that one. I reminded him that when he was on earth, he wasn't into spirituality like I was. Now here he was, teaching me.

18

IN MY WILDEST DREAMS

I have to admit, I became a little obsessed with finding answers. I wanted to learn all the different ways to peer beyond the physical world of matter into the unseen realms of mystery, to find a way to meet my husband. In my spare time, I committed myself to diving as deeply as possible into my studies. I began with my dreamtime since I had heard it was often easier to connect to Spirit during sleep.

In books on dream interpretation, I discovered different symbols mean different things based on our particular situations or life experiences. I came across countless experts advising dream journaling. If we record our dreams, we can start to identify different themes. I started keeping a journal where I wrote down details about dreams I had in an effort to remember them and to analyze their significance.

Ever since I was little, I've often dreamt about tigers. Much of the time, these beautiful animals are chasing me, and I am afraid of them. In one dream, I was in a strange place, a place where I knew I lived, but it looked nothing like my home. There was a baby tiger wandering around indoors. I didn't know how it had gotten there, and I didn't want to be responsible for it. I was terrified of it.

What if it hurt me, or someone else? I needed to find a cage for it. So I put the tiger in the cage and then felt guilty for capturing it. I decided the cage was too small so I got a bigger one. But that didn't feel right either. The tiger didn't belong there. Suddenly a giant snake came out of the tiger's mouth. This frightened me even more. I jumped back, and then I woke up.

Messages in our dreams are often about our subconscious interpretations. We create our own meanings for things such as animals and symbols. For me, the tiger represents personal power, and snakes relate to transformation, healing, and change. The message I took from the dream was that I was struggling to claim my personal power as I grieved Todd's death. The tiger was thrust upon me in the dream. I didn't want it, just like I hadn't wanted Todd to die. I couldn't escape it; I had to face it.

I also saw myself as the tiger because I wanted to stick myself in a little cage. I'd tried a bigger cage, but that didn't work either. I was forced to step out of my comfort zone and go through the grief process. The experience was terrifying but part of my soul's journey.

It seems that I have struggled with communication my entire life. Sometimes I bite my tongue for fear of what will happen if I speak up. So it's interesting that the snake came out of the tiger's mouth.

In the dream, I worried that I or others would get hurt. I sometimes fear that following my dreams and claiming my personal power will hurt others. Spirit always sees the bigger picture. Often I think it would feel better to hide, but stepping out of my comfort zone is necessary for transformation.

Sometimes we act with purpose and other times simply out of habit. I never wanted to ruffle any feathers as a child. I chose to be the good girl, the one who kept the peace and avoided conflict as a way to get through the chaos of childhood. My communication issues served a purpose in the past, but they have become a habit, one

I would like to break. While Todd was alive, there was never a need to address this seemingly buried issue. Now I'm discovering things about myself I didn't need to face before, things I kept beneath the surface.

Tracking dreams can lead to a lot of discovery. I noticed a direct connection between what was happening in my waking hours and the messages I received in dreams. The more I tracked my dreams, the easier it was to recall them and eventually direct them.

Psychic medium Matt Fraser writes, "Every so often your loved ones will open the door from heaven and visit you in a dream. Just to say HELLO and remind you they are still with you, just in a different way."

Many times, Todd has told Alexia to have me pay attention to my dreams because he wants to communicate with me in dreamtime. Soon, I started to see him in my dreams. In one of them, Todd and I were riding a bicycle in a beautiful countryside. He was steering the bike and holding me as we cycled past gorgeous scenery with lots of trees, grass, and winding narrow roads. I felt so light in Todd's arms as we rushed through the countryside at top speed. It was thrilling and breathtaking. Every part of me felt as if I was physically there. I could feel the breeze and the freedom of being alive. I was a little afraid because we were going so fast, but confident because I knew Todd had me. I felt completely supported, without a care in the world.

When we stopped at a café, I wanted to park the bicycle inside so no one would steal it. As I fretted about the bike, Todd went in and enjoyed breakfast. He even got a pedicure! (He was not the sort of guy to get his nails done.) Eventually, I joined him.

This is my interpretation of the dream: I'd been worried about things, and Todd was telling me that he had my back and was guiding me and carrying me on all of our adventures. I needed to trust and relax and enjoy the journey of my life. I needed to see and absorb the beauty and peace and not worry about the material things, which the bike represented. The dream was Todd's way of letting me know that in heaven all feels wonderful. On earth we worry about these things. That worry isn't helpful. It only keeps us from the joy that is always all around us, always available to us.

As I delved deeper into dream study, I discovered the practice of lucid dreaming. Basically, it's the ability to feel fully present in the dream state and to remember it afterward. The dreamer is aware that they are dreaming and may have some control over what happens in the dream, where it takes place, and who is present. It's a way to vividly experience something in the dream world. I decided to try my luck at lucid dreaming, hoping that I could connect to Todd in the dream state.

It can take a lot of practice to induce a lucid dream. Experts say the likelihood of having a lucid dream is increased by keeping a dream journal and writing down everything that happened in the dream upon waking. Another key to lucid dreaming is to question whether you're dreaming while awake and during dreams. If you question whether you are dreaming in the daytime hours, you'll get into the habit of questioning while in the dream state too. Questioning while in the dream state will remind you that you are actually in a dream state, and then you can begin to have fun and explore.

I had my first lucid dream before Todd and I moved into our dream home. While I was sleeping, I'd recognized I was dreaming and then physically felt that I was present in the dreamscape. I was standing in our bedroom, trying to figure out what to do next. I decided to make it rain. To my delight, when I peered out the picture window, it was pouring. It was intriguing and a little frightening at the same time. I didn't realize that what I had experienced was a lucid dream; I just knew it felt more real than any dream I'd ever had.

That lucid dream was the only one I'd ever had. After Todd died, it gave me hope that I could repeat the experience. After many nights of trying unsuccessfully to reach that state, one night I finally found myself questioning whether I was awake or sleeping in the dream state. I looked around and things looked a little different than normal. I walked into a room full of people in an unfamiliar house. I recognized my grandfather and said to him, "Grandpa, you're dead."

I realized I was dreaming and ran frantically through the house looking for Todd. He was sitting in another room on a burgundy couch with some people who seemed familiar even though I haven't met them in this lifetime. Todd and I embraced and kissed.

Almost immediately, I could feel myself waking up. I tried spinning around, which is one way to stay grounded in a lucid dream. It didn't work. I woke up. I lay in bed thinking, what just happened? I was grateful I'd seen Todd, but I felt cheated. I'd awakened too soon. I wanted more time with my husband. I resolved to practice more and get better at lucid dreaming. I couldn't wait for nighttime to come so I could try it again.

19

THE BEAUTY OF TRANSFORMATION

In the early days following Todd's death, I needed to keep moving to survive. As the years went by, I started to view moving forward in a different light. It meant working toward a balance of work and play and figuring out how to not just continue living but to thrive. Through my loss, I learned the vital importance of relationships. Nothing is as important as spending time with the people and the animals we love.

I've surrounded myself with a tribe of friends and family that not only support me but have my back. I've come to learn just how valuable and precious these relationships are. There is nothing like death to make us realize in profound ways that nothing matters more than each other. It's the love. It's always been the love.

I've also learned that being vulnerable and opening up to people lets us experience the pureness of love in deeper, more profound ways. When we open ourselves up and share ourselves and we're trusted with the same openness in return, we can be real with one another, and we learn just how similar we are. We are okay with being ourselves and sharing our raw emotions.

I'd already begun to take steps toward living more vibrantly again when I attended the "I Can Do It" conference in Florida, a weekend of learning from many extraordinary spiritual leaders, including Anita Moorjani and Wayne Dyer, both of whom I admired.

My friend Jese joined me on the trip. We got settled into our hotel room, which had a wonderful view of the ocean. Jese wanted to rest after the flight, so I went for a walk. I took in the wooden boardwalk and the sky as I strolled, soaking up the warmth of the Florida sunshine. A man in orange shorts and sandals walked toward me. To my utter surprise, I recognized him. It was Wayne Dyer, the keynote speaker for the conference. One of the items on my bucket list was to meet him. I'd read several of his books when I was younger. Now there he was, coming straight toward me!

My voice shook as I introduced myself and told him I was attending the conference. He asked where I was from, and we chatted briefly. I told him about Todd's passing and about how much his teachings had meant to me through the years. He had such a calm, peaceful energy, I could see instantly that he moved through life completely present in every moment.

I couldn't wait to get back to the hotel room and call Alexia to tell her about my encounter. I called Becky, too. She said it was no chance meeting. It had happened for a reason, and Todd had been right there. I'd known instinctively that my husband had a hand in the meeting. Every day there is a new sign from Todd to show me the magic in living.

Jese and I were on our way to supper the second evening of the conference when a woman got on the elevator with us. It was Anita Moorjani. Jumping at my chance I said, "Anita, I've read your book, and I can't tell you how much it meant to me."

She smiled at me kindly, so I went on.

"Your description of heaven and everything you went through is so inspiring." I told her about Todd and how her book and message had helped me.

Compassion shone in Anita's eyes. "Your husband is with you all the time," she said. "He's here now and will always be with you." We reached the ground floor and parted when the elevator doors opened. Jese looked at me and said quizzically, "What just happened?"

I nervously sputtered, "That was the lady who wrote the book I was telling you about, *Dying to Be Me.*"

Jese was excited for me. We couldn't believe I'd gotten to meet both Anita and Wayne. What divine timing!

In January of 2015, I took Alexia to the "I Am Light" conference in Maui, featuring both Wayne Dyer and Anita Moorjani. I knew the conference would be healing, and it was. We savored two days of workshops, meditation, and words of wisdom from Wayne Dyer, Anita Moorjani, Scarlett Lewis, and Immaculee Libagiza, all of whom had suffered and learned from tremendous losses. Alexia still talks about the peace that came over the two of us as we took long walks on the beach, reflecting on Todd and on moving forward.

Listening to Wayne Dyer talk was more than inspiring. He seemed to speak effortlessly about the power of love as he connected to the rapt audience. He said, "There's an invisible intelligence that is keeping the planets in alignment, that is opening all of the flowers every morning, that is growing your fingernails. We are all the same, all a part of the same force, all a part of love."

After Wayne and the other speakers finished, everyone got in line to meet Wayne and to have him sign books. I was grateful that I got to meet him again but more grateful that Alexia would meet him. I wanted her to experience his peaceful presence.

I told Wayne about Todd, and I asked him if he would give Alexia a big fatherly hug. As he did so, he held her hand up and said, "Look at your nails, they grow everyday just like mine do." I was grateful that he was affirming to her that we are all a part of that same beautiful force of love.

Attending these conscious awareness conferences was invigorating. Through them, I discovered the beauty of aligning with higher energy and allowing the universe to bring me whatever I need at any given moment. I also learned on a deeper level that death doesn't really exist. Not the way I used to think it did. We never really die; we transform. The message was strong: We are all one. We're never separated from any of our loved ones.

20

DO WHAT FEELS RIGHT

In the fall of 2014, I was finally ready to begin offering hypnosis sessions. Becky had always dreamed of having a healing center, and I couldn't think of anyone with whom I'd rather collaborate. We rented a small, three-room space with a small waiting area in Northfield, Minnesota. It was a dream come true.

We named the space The Inspiration Nook. Becky said inspiration means in-Spirit, and our place was small, so Inspiration Nook seemed like the perfect name. I decided to call my hypnosis business Beautiful Day Hypnosis in honor of Todd. He used to always say, "Isn't it a beautiful day?" It seemed like a great name for such a beautiful healing modality.

Anxiety set in as we unpacked and got the healing rooms set up. I was nervous about working with clients. What if I wasn't any good at it? I recalled how profoundly Devin had helped me heal from the trauma when Carmel was injured. Devin had taught me that all hypnosis is self-hypnosis. Our thoughts, feelings, and beliefs all work together. We can change the things that don't work in our lives anymore by changing our limiting beliefs. I wanted to teach others how to heal themselves. I promised myself I wasn't going to let self-doubt and fear get in my way.

Just then Becky said, "There goes Todd through the doorway into your room."

"You see him?" I asked, incredulous.

She replied, "I see his energy signature. He just swept past you."

Todd's presence fortified me. It made me eager to guide others to healing. From the start, I felt him and my angels and guides by my side, my invisible team working to help others with hypnosis so they could learn to heal through meditation. It was time for me to take all the tools I'd learned from my journey through pain and grief and offer that experience to others who were still suffering.

First, I practiced on friends and family. When it came time to work with the public, panic rose in me. I couldn't sleep the night before my first client. I thought I would throw up. I got such anxiety that I didn't think I could make it through the session. My voice would start to crack, and I would wonder what business I had thinking I could do this. Old tapes played in my mind: "Brenda, you're not good enough." Doubt not only knocked at the door—it broke the door down.

Motivational speaker Brian Tracy says, "There are no limits to what you can accomplish, except the limits you place on your own thinking." I kept this in mind every time I felt tempted to give in to my negative self-talk. I could feel Todd encouraging me and hear him tell me, "It will get easier." He was right. Every time I did a session, it got a little easier. I started out using my notes and scripts and eventually learned to listen to Spirit direct me through the session. When I eased into it and listened for guidance, the words flowed easily and naturally.

I knew I was on the right path. Eventually, I felt a sense of peace during the sessions, which led me to believe in myself and in my ability to let Spirit speak through me. I think the people who come in for sessions are warriors. It takes courage to do the work. Once they've experienced hypnosis and the ease that comes with it, they can tap into the practices on their own without my guidance.

One of my favorite ways to use hypnosis is for past life regression and future life progression. As the weeks turned into months, I became increasingly comfortable with this work. Every time I worked with a client, I felt like I was living my purpose.

In 2016, I stumbled on a training for Quantum Healing Hypnosis Technique (QHHT). In QHHT, a method discovered by hypnotherapist Delores Cannon, a practitioner guides a client through past-life regressions and then has a conversation with the client's Higher Self (also called the Collective Consciousness).

Using QHHT is like taking someone on time travel. Facilitators teach people to communicate with their Higher Self for their greatest and highest good. Clients experience memories and feelings from when their soul lived a different lifetime. This allows them to release old wounds and trauma that may be hindering their current happiness and well-being.

I decided I had to take the training. I wanted to help people get in touch with their higher selves. I got the message from Todd that it would be good to expand my training, so I took another leap of faith and traveled to the Level One training in Arkansas and the Level Two training in Canada. Todd was there with me. He joked, "I get to train with you."

I found that miraculous things can happen with QHHT. One gentleman told me prior to our session that he experienced debilitating pain in his legs and back. This kept him from doing things he enjoyed, like taking walks with his wife. During the session, he asked for healing in his legs and back and gave himself permission to heal in these areas. He was astonished when he stood up following the session and immediately noticed greater ease with walking and significantly less pain in his back and legs.

Todd has helped me step onto my healing path. He's taught me to follow my instincts. Spirit is always guiding us and inspiring us to be the best versions of ourselves. Living an inspired life leads us to our heart's desires, our destiny.

Sometimes the most difficult step is discerning what we truly want. Todd was an expert at this, in my opinion. He was like a child at play, totally absorbed in the present and taking things one moment at a time. If I could go back in time, I wouldn't worry so much about the bills or the things that needed to get done. I'd get lost in play with Todd more often. Those times we just talked or looked at the stars together or slept outside on the deck with the kids in the summer are the times I felt deep joy. That's what Todd felt most of the time, what I believe we are all meant to feel every day.

For many of us, our thoughts seem wrong, and our emotions don't feel good much of the time. We grow older and stop doing the things we love to do. Worse, we stop trusting ourselves to make the right decisions. We don't listen to our instincts. We end up feeling stuck. When people reach the end of their lives, they don't typically think about their big houses or their 9-to-5 jobs. They recall the joy they experienced with their loved ones.

For years, Todd had urged me to learn hypnosis because he knew it was important to me. I'd wanted to explore it for most of my life, but it's easy to forget our deepest longings. Our egos drive us toward earthly concerns, like worrying about money or what other people will think. We forget that when we pursue what we came here for, the universe will work with us to make it happen.

Once I completed the coursework for QHHT, I talked to Becky. "I don't know Becky. I'm not sure I can do this. I'm afraid I won't be any good at it." She grinned, "Nonsense, you'll be great. They are telling me you are a natural, and I know it too." She told me it would get easier the more I practice and get over my fear, the same way it had when I first did hypnosis sessions. She had me do a session on her, and I was also practicing with family and friends. When I was closer to feeling ready, she sent people my way just like she did with the other hypnosis sessions.

Like Becky and my guides had said, I started to feel more and more comfortable with the process the more I did it. I discovered I especially liked forming a relationship with those I worked with and seeing them make the positive changes they desired and shifts in their perception and focus.

At the beginning of a hypnosis session, we discuss what they want to work on, such as getting rid of limiting beliefs about themselves and the changes they are ready to make. My hypnosis teacher, Devin, taught me that we all need to have significant reasons for the things we want to change in order for the changes to happen. When we are ready to make change, we can effectively work on our thoughts, beliefs, feelings, and behaviors to make the changes we desire. All the changes are available to us—and in us—but no one can do our inner work for us. As a hypnotherapist, I'm just there to guide clients to their growth and alignment.

Practice really does make perfect. I've noticed the more a person meditates, the quicker they can relax, align, and go within. That's where the real healing and manifesting process is.

During a session with Alexia, she described a feeling of being stuck. She told me she felt burdened about being her age and feeling that she hadn't accomplished what she felt she should have by now. We talked about her feelings and how her mind and ego play a part in these feelings. I reminded her how her dad used to tell her to "stop being so hard on yourself."

At this point, she had already done numerous sessions with me, and she could easily and quickly get into a relaxed hypnotic state. We started the session the way we usually did, by deep breathing. I then had Alexia enter and immerse herself in her beautiful garden.

She began experiencing the freedom of being with her father in the summertime. She felt the sunshine on her face, the light breeze, and a pageantry of beautiful colors around her. I asked her to step backward in time, and she found herself on a path that led her to a long hallway. In that hallway, there were rows and rows of doors of all different shapes, sizes, and colors. She then picked out the door that she felt drawn to. She chose a large green wooden door with lots of intricate carvings on it. Each door represented different lifetimes—some from the past and some from the future.

She opened the green door and immediately told me she was standing before a beautiful, old, white colonial home. As she moved inside the house, she could feel her long curls bounce around her neck as she walked forward. She looked down at her dress and noticed it was bluish with lace; she felt constricted and told me it was because she was wearing a corset. She held up her dress revealing bloomers and tall black boots.

She told me she felt young and pretty. She could hear her boots clicking against the wooden floor as she walked down the hall that was lined with old portraits of people she sensed were familiar to her. "Mom, I know the people in these pictures; they are family!" She could hear the creaks again from the floor and her own heels as she made her way down the hallway.

As she moved into other rooms, she described the layout to me. She added, "I smell the staleness and leather." The house was large and filled with nice things that mostly looked weathered. She said it was a very nice house in its time.

As I directed her to a significant period in that lifetime, she teared up, "I am very close to my uncle. He is like a father to me." She said, "Actually my uncle is more of a father to me than my own." She smiled, "It's Dad, he is my uncle." Todd was her uncle in this lifetime, and this was the first of many lifetimes she would have with him. I was taken aback by how special this message was for her. Tears poured from her eyes as I handed her a tissue.

She told me that his role was very important in this lifetime. He helped her stand up for herself and to always do what was right, even if it was difficult. She was without children in this lifetime. She fought for women's rights. She was an influential woman who was respected by her peers in the community. She worked hard and wasn't afraid to let people know that men and women deserve equal rights.

I then directed her to another significant period in this lifetime. "I'm lying on a bed; I'm old and dying," she said. "Everyone I love is here." She felt the love they had for her and the love she felt for them. While viewing the scene, she said she knew she was ready to die because her life felt complete. She went on to tell me after the session that her soul's work was done. She had accomplished what she set out to do in this lifetime. Even though she was sad about not having children, she knew the students she looked after were like her own children to her. And it all transpired the way it was supposed to.

As she blinked her eyes open after the session, she said, "I feel so good, Mom. Dad was with me, just like he is now. Dad wants me to remember that I am capable of whatever I want to do in my life, and there is nothing to fear, I can't get it wrong."

A few days later, Alexia told me that session helped her to not be afraid of death. She said knowing Todd had been with her before and will be with her again helps her understand we will all be together again. She added, "I know Dad came through like that to let me know I shouldn't be afraid of doing what I want in this life; I should pursue my dreams and live life in the present."

In another session, this time with friend Michelle, I observed and guided her to go back in time, and she viewed several memories from her childhood. She had fond memories of her grandfather, intertwined with some distressing memories of her biological mom.

Prior to the session, Michelle and I talked about her need to declutter her home of boxes and stacks of material possessions that she had been acquiring throughout her life. She told me that she needed to rid herself of these items because it was getting hard to navigate through her home, and she wanted to be free of the need to keep these things, some of which were sentimental. She told me she was torn, not wanting to part with the items but also not wanting to have them take over her any longer.

In between her beautiful memories of sitting on her grandpa's lap, singing with him and helping him on the family farm (the same farm she now owns and stores her possessions in), were memories of her mom.

In one memory, she clearly recalled being locked in the cold, dark basement while her mom was kissing a man that was not her father. She was scared while reviewing the memory. She banged on the basement door with all her strength and pleaded, "Mother, let me out!" But no response came.

As Michelle went from memories of this childhood to a past life in which she was alone and barely existing, she made a connection. She doesn't have to be lonely in this life. The things (possessions) aren't really needed anymore. They might have been needed at one time to get her through a time that was really scary, when she couldn't depend on her mother to keep her safe and she had to find a way to survive the trauma.

She had unconsciously drawn a connection between her grandparents' belongings that she inherited with the security they provided. She didn't want to part with the possessions because they were connected to her grandparents and the security she felt with them. She began to see that her stacks of possessions were there as a wall of protection on an unconscious level.

Now she is releasing the need to have these possessions for protection. As an adult, she can stand up for herself and defend herself; as a child, she was unable to. So she is honoring and standing up for herself and the child in her that still needs protection.

Oftentimes, we don't realize the patterns we create when we're young that help us function in the world. As an adult, we don't need them anymore. We can choose differently.

I'm amazed by how guides and angels always direct the sessions where they need to go. The amount of healing and guidance is so abundant. I love and feel honored to be in attendance of this divine energy.

21

ALIGNING WITH MY HIGHER SELF

We continually align with our purpose, get off track, and then are redirected into alignment through inspiration from our higher selves, angels, guides, and loved ones on the other side. I get so much pleasure from guiding people into connection with their higher selves through hypnosis sessions. I'm really excited about the next spiritual learning adventure the universe will point me towards.

One of the ways I stay aligned with my life purpose is by taking walks in nature and talking to my Higher Self. One day, I asked my Higher Self, "Why is it so hard to complete my goals? Why do I feel like it's taking so long to get where I want to go?"

My Higher Self answered:

You chose to come to earth. In doing so, you feel separated from your real self. You don't feel whole; you don't feel light. You see things differently there than we do. We can see the big picture of your plan for this lifetime.

The world can be overwhelming. You sometimes get clear enough to see how you want things to go but can't necessarily feel the way you want them to go. You have a higher purpose and work toward your goals continuously. However, you still need to attend to your life, including paying bills, doctors' visits, remembering a friend's birthday, etc.

You feel like you don't have enough time. The more you work toward your higher goals the more time you will have. When you raise your vibration and align with who you really are, there is no time.

Your focus is so important. Get more clear about what you really want and concentrate on it. And yes, you will still have time for the things in life that you feel have to get done. The truth is, you have more than enough time, you just don't believe you do.

Do anything that raises your vibration. When you feel good, you are able to get many things done. It's not that you suddenly have more time available. The time was always there ,but you were focused on not having enough of it.

Whenever I connect with my Higher Self, it gives me the following message: *Do what feels right. Be light and live in joy.* When we live in the moment with passion, everything falls magically into place. My life has changed for the better as I've aligned more and more with my Higher Self. I'm still amazed by the thoughts that come when I ask for guidance. I've worked hard to listen to my gut and go with what feels right. The Higher Self is always directing us to the light, if we pay attention.

Yoga is another practice for raising our awareness. I recently joined a yoga studio in a soothing loft setting, with wood floors, brick walls, salt lamps, candles, and singing bowls. Yoga eases my physical pain and also quiets my mind. It's a lovely combination. My amazing teacher Tracy is the essence of peace as she leads students into the quiet spaces of our souls while stretching our limbs. She ends classes with calming touch and essential oils. The studio is filled with the tones of a gong vibrating off the floor, walls, and ultimately reaching the interiors of our souls.

I often connect with Todd in *savasana*, the reflective state at the end of class. We meet in a boat on the river. He is either looking at me and rowing or holding me as I stretch my arm out to feel the water. Sometimes I imagine the two of us eating peanut butter sandwiches and drifting quietly in the night. I think it's Todd being humorous; he always loved peanut butter sandwiches. Other times we meet family members from the other side on the dock.

Practicing yoga helps my body feel free. My mind and heart fill with healing energy and peace. It's a great way to practice the art of self-love and align with my Higher Self.

22

PIERCING THE VEIL

As the days and weeks following Todd's death turned into years, instead of the bond between us fraying, I felt closer to my husband as I used all the tools I had to connect with his spirit. The times I connected with Todd in my dreams made me so excited. Not only could I talk with him during waking hours, but I could expand my awareness and be with him during sleep.

After my experience with lucid dreaming, I felt more confident about stepping into other realms. I was fascinated by astral travel. I hardly dared to hope that I could travel out of my body and find Todd in the spiritual realm, but I was eager to bridge the gap between us to be with Todd in any way possible.

In astral travel, the soul or consciousness separates from the physical body and moves up and away from it, making it possible to explore other spiritual realms and dimensions. We naturally travel out of our bodies during the night, but we don't remember doing so.

It takes some practice to relax the body while keeping the mind alert. It's sort of like tricking yourself into thinking you're asleep while you're hyper-aware of being conscious. It can be hard to maintain that state while your body is so relaxed because you automatically want to fall asleep.

There are many ways to induce astral travel. One is to visualize walking through your house while you are resting, keeping your body still and the mind awake. You imagine your physical body exploring your home, using all of your senses as you move about the rooms. For example, you might imagine the feeling of the floor under your feet and the texture of the kitchen counters and cabinets as you reach out and touch them.

Astral travel is easy for some people, but I found it difficult at first. A lot of times, I fell asleep before I could get out of my body. I'd wake up feeling frustrated but tried not to let it discourage me. I was determined to find a way to meet Todd in the memorial garden in the backyard. Todd had told Alexia this would be a good place for us to meet because he loves going there.

After many nights of trying, I finally broke through. I lay completely still, trying not to move a muscle. I focused on my breath and then tuned into the energy in the room, which had a faint buzzing sound. I tried not to think of anything, just like I do when I meditate. After what seemed like forever, the buzzing grew louder. I sensed vibrations pulsing and movement, almost like going through a tunnel on a train. There was a pulling sensation as I exited my body.

I found myself standing in my bedroom. I still felt like I had a body, but I was floating through air. I was free and excited that I'd made it. I could touch things and move around the rooms. I glided through the house, exploring. Everything looked slightly different. I was in my house, but the furnishings were arranged differently. There were lots of vivid colors, richer and deeper than usual. I was able to pass through the kitchen door without opening it. I went outside and levitated up into the night sky. As I flew around, it felt magical, like anything was possible.

The next thing I knew, it was morning. I was back in my body, in bed. But I remembered that I'd been out. I had done it! I hadn't found Todd, but it was a start. I had hope that I could meet him somewhere in between the physical and the heavenly realms.

I lay in bed thinking about what it must be like for Todd to be able to explore the entire universe and to be everywhere at once. It reminded me of the trip we'd taken to Las Vegas the year before Todd passed. It was his first airplane ride, and it had taken a lot of convincing to get him comfortable with flying. He was so nervous he gripped the armrests as the plane took off. I reminded him to breathe and chuckled to myself as he braced himself in his seat.

We had gone to the Chris Angel magic show at the Luxor. We'd watched his TV show "Mind Freak" for years and marveled at his stunts. Todd was in awe when we saw Angel perform live. He clapped louder and prouder than any other fan when Angel levitated off the stage. Todd and I had talked about what it would be like to levitate. I'd told him maybe we could levitate if we truly believed it was possible.

I couldn't wait to try to astral travel again the next night. I thought about the magical things that could happen if I believed just a little. It's an infinite universe, after all. Several nights went by with no success. I would either fall asleep or make it to my living room only to wake up before I could get through the basement and out into the backyard. I felt like giving up, but reminded myself that anything worthwhile takes practice.

The next night I settled into bed, excited to try again. I wanted to move my body and go to sleep, but I hung on. Finally, I felt my essence pulling up from my body and heard loud sensations just like the first time. I made my way to the living room. Everything looked vivid and slightly different again, so I knew I was astral traveling. I reached for the door to the basement then caught myself and floated through it. I floated all the way downstairs, through the basement door, and out into the backyard near the memorial garden in search of Todd.

He was standing there in his work jeans and the blue t-shirt I loved so much. He put his arms around me and I felt the weight of him as if he was back in human form. I could even smell him.

Finally, Todd was with me again.

I wanted the moment to last forever. I couldn't believe how real it was. It felt like the many times we'd sat together at the end of the day on a bench outside or on the living room couch, where he'd pull my socks off one at a time and massage my feet. Or like the times we rode on the Ferris wheel because it was the only ride we could get ourselves to do for the kids. We'd hold each other tightly because we were both scared to death.

I wished I could stay in that moment in between space and time with Todd forever. Just as quickly as I thought it, I awoke in my bed. But unlike the other days, I could take the feeling of Todd with me into my day.

Over the next few weeks, I tried to meet Todd again, but I always fell asleep. In the mornings, I awoke feeling frustrated that I'd missed another opportunity. One night when I looked at the clock, it was after three a.m., but I was determined to go out again. I tuned into the vibrations running through me and around me as I listened to the sound of the energy. I succeeded for a few moments before I found myself back in my bed.

I finally got through and was floating downstairs to the basement when the alarm sounded. I rolled over to shut it off and found myself back in my body in bed. I tried immediately to get out again and made it. I was in my bedroom looking out the window at the backyard, which like the house, looked similar, but different. I made it to the backyard, where I noticed a huge garden building structure that intrigued me. Todd was standing near it, clearing the weeds. He gave me a big smile, gathered me in his strong arms, and kissed me eagerly. We held each other a little while, and just like that, I woke up, wishing I could stay with Todd forever.

I found myself smiling throughout the day. I'd had time with my husband! It was real and so marvelous. I walked through the day excited about our time together and all the possibilities and connections yet to come.

23

TOGETHER FOREVER

As I continued to practice astral travel, I was able to reach the backyard more and more. Todd was always there waiting for me. Sometimes we talked to one another, and other times, we just held each other. Then suddenly, for several nights, I couldn't travel. I felt frustrated. I was having such a difficult time getting through. Then, Alexia told me that Todd would help me get out of my body.

Later that night, he did just that. I was trying really hard, focusing on the energy in the room, keeping my body still while I waited for the humming sound. Just as I started to feel my spirit exit my body, I felt Todd's hand pulling me out. I made my way to the garden with him.

One night I had several astral projections. Todd had a glow around him, and his eyes were more vividly hazel than they'd been when he was alive. I felt butterflies seeing him. During the next astral travel, I found Todd standing over by the barn, fixing his black Dodge pickup truck. He was wearing his blue t-shirt again, the one that I loved. When he saw me, he put down his tools and came running toward me. The next thing I knew, I was back in my body, waking up. I tried to get back to Todd but couldn't.

As morning drew near, I felt Todd's breath in my ear and his arms around me. Five-year- old Jackson had spent the night and was sleeping beside me. I felt Todd's energy move into the space between us in the bed.

Later that morning, Jackson woke excitedly. He told me he'd been in a park with Grandpa Todd. It was nighttime in the park, and they were going to eat popsicles. "I woke up too soon, Grandma!" He exclaimed. "We didn't get to eat the popsicles!"

Another nighttime visit happened on the eve of our wedding anniversary, nearly a year after Todd died. I had been struggling more than usual with the start of summer, the gorgeous weather, and not having Todd there to enjoy our beautiful home. I was tossing and turning in the middle of the night, when I saw and felt my husband next to me. He was holding me. He looked like himself, only he was bathed in pure glowing golden energy. He seemed just the same as when he was alive. He felt *real*.

My dear husband held me in his magnificent light. It was a long, amazing embrace. He told me telepathically that he was there for me and always would be. I will never forget that visit. Todd glowed with light, but he was in his physical form. There was absolutely no difference in his touch. It felt like it always did. I didn't want it to end. I woke feeling so appreciative in the morning, so grateful for our connection.

When I told Becky about it, she said with a big smile, "You had a visit from Todd! It wasn't just a dream, it was a *visit*. He came to let you know he's still with you and he loves you. He says, "Happy anniversary, sweetheart."

That is just what he would have said, those very words.

The kids and I spent Mother's Day 2017 at Todd's parents' house. Jackson and I sat on the swing in the backyard, talking about life and Grandpa Todd. I told Jackson that I'd been seeing daisies all day, and I believed Grandpa was sending them to me as signs.

Jackson nodded. "He's with me, too, Grandma. He's here now, sitting with us."

I hugged my grandson and told him how nice it was to be with him and Todd. He hugged me back and then slid further away from me. Grandpa needed a little more room.

Later that afternoon, Alexia, Jackson, and Dakota gave me a Mother's Day gift. Alexia pointed out something she'd written on the card that was from Todd. It read, "Hey there beautiful, remember to stop and smell the daisies. They're for you. Love you for eternity."

24

BEING THE LOVE YOU SEEK

Growing up, I didn't have great examples of healthy, loving marital relationships. I certainly didn't see them in my own family. But, I knew what one looked like or what one should look like. And, I knew what a marriage shouldn't look like. So, I knew what I didn't want in a relationship.

My mom felt trapped in her marriage to my father until she finally and courageously gave herself permission to divorce him. That happened much later, after I graduated from high school. My father spent his remaining time on earth wishing he could still be with her; he called her "the love of his life." Having endured the physical and emotional abuse from him, she never wanted to go back to him. However, she forgave him, but he never forgave himself.

Although there were small pleasant memories of laughter and joy, the majority of what I remember was his constant ridicule and anger toward her and toward us. What seemed like a long time for me must have seemed like an eternity to Mom.

Many of my childhood years were spent at my grandparent's farm. Grandpa Algot and Grandma Myra slept in separate bedrooms. He slept in a little room off the dining room that barely had enough room for his bed, lamp, and nightstand for his books. She slept on the fold- out couch in the living room. Looking back now, it seemed like they did little better than tolerate one another.

I remember when my grandpa would come in after a long day of work on the farm. He would open the screen door, take off his boots, unstrap one of his bib overall straps, wash up, and eat the meal my grandma prepared for him and the rest of us. There was no kiss hello, no warm inviting looks or expressions of love. They seemingly went about their days on their own without connection.

Of course, I'd seen enough examples of loving relationships on television to know they existed somewhere, just not here. I knew I wanted more than what I had seen through family patterns. I knew there was more.

We don't have to live the way others have lived just because it's familiar to us. We don't have to repeat the patterns of the past. Instead, we can create the love we want with our loving focus, intent, and joy.

People would often ask me and Todd what our secret was. "You are so lucky to have had such a love; it is rare." I don't think it should be a secret or rare. We can either bring out the best in each other or the worst. The "secret" is you must love the way you want to be loved. You have to give what you want to receive.

Allow your loved one to be themselves, and just enjoy each other. Love each other's greatness and flaws. Give and receive. There is a balance and a need to hold this person in high regard. Those around you know the depths of your love not only because they can see it, but because they can feel it. To have this kind of love is to give this kind of love. There is no secret. I am this kind of love, and so is Todd. And so is EVERYONE.

Love is meant to be freeing. Your partner wants the best for you, and you want the best for them. You want them to pursue their dreams; you're excited to see them living their best life. We each need to feel a sense of freedom to be ourselves, to explore our interests, and to enrich each other's lives, both together and individually. This is why freedom is so integral in a deep, loving connection.

Well-meaning friends and family have also said, "You will never find this kind of love again. Todd WAS the love of your life." When I hear those words, I cringe.

I'm not buying into this limited view of love. First of all, it's not lost. Todd is still with me. And secondly, love can't be limited. One of the most beautiful things is knowing just how happy Todd wants me to be. My heart is big. It's huge and unstoppable. If I choose to love this way again, I will. In fact, I won't settle for less. It must be big, all-encompassing, expansive love, or why bother? A love that is full and continually growing. And it will be full of freedom.

Todd had this saying. He used to tell me, "You're so good to me." We were good to each other and therefore good for each other. Simple as that. Loving relationships are composed of two people loving each other in all ways and always. This respect and love made me feel accepted and valued, giving me the freedom and power to grow. There were lots of examples of times we gave each other the freedom to grow, individually and together.

I remember my brother Adrian telling me something after Todd's passing. He told me how sweet it was when Todd wanted to run things by me. He said when Todd's friends and Adrian would plan fishing trips together, Todd would always say, "I have to run it by Brenda." The truth is, I always said okay to whatever plans he had with the guys. Nevertheless, Todd still said, "I'll run it by Brenda." The guys would tease him and say things like, "Oh, you can't make a decision without her." It didn't bother him one bit. Todd would just smile and say, "I'm sure it will work out, but I first have to run it by Brenda."

I was happy when he did things that he loved to do. There is nothing greater than seeing someone you love doing what excites them. I saw that when he would work with the horses or ride his motorcycle. He was always encouraged to be himself, and he knew so completely how to live in that joy.

LOVE IS FREEING.

25

THE SOUL GROWS

All things happen for reasons we may not understand. There is a bigger plan for each of us. Experiences necessary for soul growth are going to happen, whether in this lifetime or another. But time is precious. We should do the things that truly make us happy, like spending time with people who make us laugh. Sometimes we are our own worst critics, doubting our decisions and making things harder than they need to be.

Spirit sees the bigger picture and reminds us that we are perfect as we are—pure light no matter what we do or don't do. We can be our own worst critics, doubting our decisions and making things harder than they need to be. We need to free ourselves from the notion that we are going to make the wrong choices and instead go with what feels right instinctively. There *is* no wrong choice.

Spiritual teacher Matt Kahn says, "What we blame, we give our power to." I've thought about this a lot. Blaming ourselves, someone else, or our situation, keeps us stuck. If I only did this or that, then things would be different. If I'd waited another minute with Todd that morning, would he still be here? If we hadn't moved, would he still be here?

It's up to us to keep moving on our paths, to fill ourselves with love by loving ourselves. Then we can move forward. We can choose how to respond when something unimaginable or life-changing happens. We grieve, but we have to keep living. We decide how we interpret our life events. In the book *Dying to be Me*, Anita Moorjani's primary message is to live fearlessly. We are meant to source our lives from love, not fear.

I've always considered myself temperamental, subject to my mercurial emotions. I didn't understand how strong I was before Todd's passing. His death showed me that I'm stronger than I believed myself to be and that I can impact how I feel by choosing my thoughts and where I place my mental focus. We are all divine souls capable of working miracles. Sometimes I'm surprised by the emotions that come up. I think that I should be past some of them by now. But grief moves through us unpredictably, on its own timeline. Some days I need to draw on more support than others.

The death of a loved one can shake us to our very core. I do my best to keep busy and put on a brave face. It's in the quiet times that I want Todd and our life together back so badly it hurts. Some days the grief is bigger than my determination to survive and carry on the way Todd would want me to. It's so strong that the only thing I want to do is join him.

I try to remember that I can choose how to use the time I have here. I can remain stuck in sadness, or I can heal my grief and honor the beautiful life I had with Todd. Our loved ones want us to feel hope. They want us to live life to the fullest. To do so, we have to go through our grief; we can't go around our feelings. By opening our hearts, we honor the beauty of life itself. There is a reason we are still alive. I'm determined to let go of my sorrow and embrace whatever life holds for me next. I don't have to say goodbye to Todd to do that. But I do need to be present to what shows up in my life.

Death teaches us that every day is precious, that we need to let go of pain, guilt, and suffering and live our lives with no regrets. I no longer fear death like I used to. I know when the time is right, I will transition and that Todd will be the first to welcome me. We are all going to our true home someday. There is nothing to fear. It's a joyous event.

What would our lives be like if we stopped resisting and allowed it to unfold? There is a lot to be grateful for. Our loved ones, our homes, the natural beauty of the planet, good health. Yet it's easy to become complacent and lose sight of what's right in front of us. When someone we love transitions, we are reminded of all that we value. It's the love we hold in our hearts for each other that matters the most. Death teaches us that. Those we love on the other side don't want us to think of them with sorrow, but rather to remember them with love, gratitude, and joy.

My husband used to say, "Brenda, don't be so hard on yourself." I've always had high expectations for myself, and while I think it's good to have high standards, it's cruel to judge oneself harshly. Todd always encouraged me to be as kind to myself as I was to others. I struggle sometimes to overcome the voice from childhood that says I'm not good enough, not worthy.

Even now, Todd is teaching me to take care of myself. He has helped me see my gifts, talents, and abilities. Many of the healing modalities I've learned, such as hypnosis, connecting to my Higher Self, and yoga, are an extension of self-love. I can hear Todd prompting me along with my angels and guides, giving me direction, cheering me on. Sometimes if I listen closely, I can hear applause, cheers, even fireworks from the other side. My soul team says, "Go for it. Do what makes you happy." I try to stay positive, to make the best of every situation. We are meant to live fully and happily most of the time.

26

LETTING GO

One day, when I was having a difficult time tending to the horses, Dakota said, "Mom, you're not a horse person. You want to be, but you're not." He was right. Dakota has always been my truth teller; it's one of his many gifts. For the longest time, tending Abby and Carmel was good therapy for me. I talked and sang to them in the evenings. But horses were Todd's passion, not mine. My burning desire is to help people heal through meditation and hypnosis. I loved the horses, and I loved spending time with them, but they were a lot of work. And they deserved more than I was willing to give them.

I thought back to Annie and Mae, Todd's team of Belgian horses for whom I'd found a home shortly after Todd died. They were so large and needed more care than I could give them. Todd had led me to the perfect people for the team, Lori, a hospice counselor, and her husband, Brian. I told Lori how hard it was to part with Todd's cherished team. Brian had always wanted a team of Belgian horses, and the couple had a beautiful farm on many acres for Annie and Mae to roam. Lori's face lit up as she talked about Brian's passion for having his own team.

The day Lori and Brian came to meet Annie and Mae, Lori, Alexia, and I were drawn to the center of the pasture. Annie and Mae had stopped there and were lined up in perfect formation, staring straight ahead. We all sensed they were with Todd. I knew that Todd had helped me find a good home for Annie and Mae. It was hard to give them to Lori and Brian, but it felt right deep inside. When we do what feels right, even though it is difficult, it brings us strength and contentment.

Letting go of the horses freed me to finally make changes in my home, too. For a long time, it had felt as if keeping things the way they were when Todd died might magically help him come back again. But after I learned he was still with me and that I could reach him whenever I wanted to, I didn't need to keep so many reminders of our life together anymore. Nothing could take away his presence in the dream home we'd created together. I called Alexia and asked her to box up Todd's clothing. She happily removed Todd's belongings and moved my clothes into the new space in the closet, carefully tucking the boxes containing Todd's things in the back.

As I prepared for bed that evening, my eyes landed on Todd's work pants. It had been three years since Todd died, and they were still draped over the bottom frame of our bed. I picked them up and tenderly added them to one of the boxes. I told myself it was okay, the pants were just an earthly possession. I smiled as Todd reminded me I can see him in his work pants any time I want just by closing my eyes.

I am slowly learning to be more joyful. The grief is lessening. I can smile, laugh, and feel joy like I did before with Todd. I often think back to when we first met, all the nights we spent cruising around and talking. I used to laugh at the number of Hostess cupcakes he devoured in a single sitting. It was impressive.

We had a lifetime of laughter, more than I think most people dream of having. Still, I need more. Todd wants me to laugh, and when I do, I can hear him laughing too. Even if the memories of our conversations fade, I'll never forget his jovial laugh and how it penetrated deep in me.

I recently went to the Healing Edge Expo in the Twin Cities. On my way there, I spied a gorgeous red-tailed hawk perched on the top branch of a bare tree. I took it as another confirmation that I was exactly where I needed to be. I couldn't wait to see Kristine, an intuitive I'd met the year before. To my surprise, she remembered me.

"Todd holds your hand," she said as she began the reading. She flashed a warm smile. "He even pushes down on your head to help you with your beliefs when you're worried. He senses your self-doubt and tries to 'head it off', so to speak. He believes in you."

Tears flowed from my eyes as Kristine said that I was learning to live in joy. "You came from Source, as we all do," she explained. "When light leaves Source, it enters darkness. When we come from such a beautiful place of light and love and enter darkness, it can be quite shocking and can stay with the soul." Her expression softened and compassion filled her words. "There has been darkness that has stayed with you your entire lifetime. This darkness is also known as the dark night of the soul."

She paused for a moment, then seemed to brighten as she continued channeling. "Celestial beings are lifting this darkness from you. It's okay to feel happy and lighthearted," she assured me.

I've received countless messages like this from Todd. Many times he has told me, "Brenda, you will be happy again. You will open your heart and love again. You will know when the time is right. I'll be right there helping you through your doubt. You were always so good to me, babe. You deserve to be happy."

How could I say no to that? I wish with all my heart that Todd was still alive. Nothing will ever change that. His death has been so difficult, and I can't understand it from my vantage point, but where Todd is, he sees the bigger plan for all of our souls' growth. I've come to know and trust that our journeys are unfolding in divine order. We are so much more than our bodies. We are divine light and love. When the time is right, we will meet again, in that heavenly space between lives. In the meantime, I choose to move toward being healed and happy.

I'm grateful for the things I have learned in the years since Todd passed. When I choose to see life with my shifted and expanded perception, I realize all these experiences are really gifts. Gifts that couldn't be realized before. Gifts that I could only realize once I allowed myself to go through the grieving process. Just like the conversation the kids and I had with Todd through Becky in the basement, all of us have learned lessons, and those lessons lead to growth. Todd continues to inspire me from the other side. I feel him nudging me to make the choices I most want to make. He encourages me to say no to those things I don't want to do and to seek happiness. He encourages me to live in the moment and not worry about things. Todd has inspired me to realize my dreams, and I hear him cheering me on. I feel his energy supporting me every step of the way. I am so honored that his love is so present. He has gone above and beyond for me, and I will do everything I can to pass on his legacy and keep his memory alive.

Pain and suffering are part of the experiences we choose to live through in order to grow our souls. Life is full of tragedy, pain, and disappointment, but it's also full of love and delight. I am so grateful for the life and experiences I have had. The biggest lesson I've learned is that love is all there is; everything else is an illusion.

I never imagined I would get to the place where I am now, feeling lighter and happier every day, seeing clients in my healing practice, and feeling so much gratitude for my life. I will always have Todd in my heart and look forward to the time when we will reunite in heaven. There is a beauty and a peace that exists that is beyond our wildest dreams. It can be best summed up as unconditional love. Although I can't fully understand why something so wonderful like my marriage, my physical life with Todd, was taken from me, I can honestly say I see in his passing the threads of a bigger picture.

Many people say that there is a part of you that is never healed after losing a loved one. This may be true. However, I don't see it like that. I see the beauty in the whole experience. Todd's soul guided me through this journey, and he is holding the light that continues to pull me through. The joy in me from the love I share with Todd can never be taken away. The unconditional love, appreciation, and joy will always be part of me, in my heart. I feel a new sense of courage and fearlessness, too. I choose a peaceful and joyous state of well-being more often now with each passing day.

When I hear someone saying unkind words to their loved ones, I want to put my hand on their shoulder and say, "Take it back. Tell them how much you love them and hold them close." We don't know how much time we have, but we do know how we feel for one another. Love is meant to grow and not limit us in any way.

In my quest for answers and connection with Todd, I had sessions with multiple intuitive guides. All of them shared a similar message for me from my husband: that I have a big heart, and I should keep it open to possibilities. Just as I wouldn't want Todd to be alone, he doesn't want that for me. I'm not holding Todd back in heaven, and he is not holding me back here.

I'm excited for him when he tells me about the things he's doing in heaven, like learning sacred geometry and fishing with his buddy Red, and being with his sister Kay. He watches over me and our family and guides us. Our physical life together has ended, but our journey and our love continues for eternity. It's a long-distance love that's not really as distant as one might think. Through all the changes, love continues to grow, and Todd continues to walk with me every step of the way.

LOVE FOREVER

In conclusion, there is no conclusion. As author and speaker Mike Dooley says, "Any and all forms of separation, disconnects, divides, partings, breakups, and goodbyes are temporary. Very. You'll be together far, far longer than you will ever be apart." We continue forever. There's no end to our souls and to our love stories.

From the moment I lost Todd, I repeated the words, "This doesn't make sense," over and over again. I could not wrap my brain, much less my heart, around the loss. How could someone as loving and wonderful as Todd be taken from us so tragically and unexpectedly? Why must there be pain, emptiness, sorrow? Brené Brown says, "In the absence of connection, love and belonging, there is always suffering." Which is why it's so important to hold on to the connection.

Loss is just an illusion. Nothing and no one is ever truly lost. Everything we do in life is part of a greater plan that we came here to accomplish. The only thing that matters in life is love.

We find out when we are in heaven that *everything* makes sense. I look back on my life and the lessons I've learned from growing up.

These things taught me valuable lessons. Growing up poor in a small town and having parents who struggled with mental illness led me to a greater understanding and my work in the fields of mental health and hypnosis. My restless and worried soul chose a free-spirited husband who loves me unconditionally, so I could learn to be joyful and free. My children and grandson taught me that they have their own paths, and it's okay for them to follow their internal wisdom.

All of my experiences have led me to where I am now and what I will do next. Though life has sometimes felt heavier than I ever thought possible, it's happening just as it should. There are no mistakes, only times when we feel we're off the path. We will always find our way back because the universe is on our side and will guide us there. And that is when we feel closest to Spirit.

We must learn to forgive ourselves and move forward, looking at things that come as part of the plan, good or bad. Spirit, God, the universe, doesn't judge us in the sense that we may perceive. We judge ourselves. We need to let go and move forward, doing the best we can.

Todd's life and his continued guidance is a gift to me, to our family and friends and to the universe, just the same as everyone's life is a gift. Through our experiences of great joy and sorrow, we get to experience divine love. Through the depths of that love, we discover our true purpose.

Todd's passing was a gift because Todd is a gift, whether he is physically here or here in spirit. We need to celebrate each other and never lose sight of what our loved ones mean to us. We are all going to transition from this life, but we don't die. We transition into ecstasy. Pure bliss.

What's more, we can live in that bliss now, experience our own heaven on earth by living in that joy, that love. Todd knew how.

I was led to write this book with Todd. It's been healing to write about our discoveries. I've learned that there are so many ways to connect and to continue to feel the love we share. My deepest wish is for people to connect with their loved ones on the other side and get through the grief. We all have the propensity not only to heal, but to flourish, as love guides us to where we need to go.

We can allow and honor every moment. We can close our eyes and see our beloveds, hear them and feel them carrying us to the joy that is on the other side of grief. We are never truly separated. We are always together. Nothing ever dies; it is transformed. The love is always there.

Now I'm seeing the magic happening not only in the big things in my life, but also in the small things. It's there when I get an idea in the middle of the night and when I step out of my comfort zone. I'm not only enjoying life, but I'm trying new things, experiencing the fullness of life. I'm noticing how I'm changing, evolving.

Todd is teaching me that not only can I experience beauty and fulfillment, I can also open my heart to love again. I think too many people have a skewed framework for love, and it's keeping them from the true experience of love. We don't have to settle for a relationship that is unfulfilling. Yes, there will be difficult times, but what's great is how we get through them together. A love where you're open, accepted, and cherished, despite faults, and where you want the best for each other is the only way to go. This kind of love feels good. And this kind of love grows and deepens. I'll say it again—if we want true love, we have to give true love. We have to be true love.

Wayne Dyer said, "Change the way you look at things and the things you look at change." Now, when I walk through my dining room on my way to the kitchen, I don't feel anxious walking past the doorway where I got the news that day. Todd's death was a tremendous gift of love. That is how I choose to think and feel about it. My perception. My soul experienced loss, and the loss led me to feel the depths of real connection, real love. I can think about Todd with joy in my heart. The tears don't fall like they used to.

Shannon was right all those years ago when he said, "Time is all we need now." It's been years since Todd's physical departure. Dakota's health has drastically improved. He's learning that he is strong and capable and discovering his interests in life. He will find his way, just like Todd said the day his presence sat on the basement steps. He has the heart of a lion.

Alexia has been fighting her own health challenges, but she, too, is realizing just how strong she really is. Todd always told her what a wonderful mom she is. She's continuing to explore her psychic abilities and is foster her creative side, which shows in her projects and homemaking. Both our children have grown into kind, loving adults with big hearts. I know Todd is proud of them. Our grandson is growing up, and he has the biggest smile and mountains of energy. He has a lot of love for his mom and wants to be a builder.

Becky and I have ventured apart in our businesses, but she continues to do healing work, touching the lives of many. We will forever remain friends and find time to get together and stay connected.

Through the depth of Todd's love, I discovered myself. Once we truly understand that we are all flawed and beautiful at the same time, we can grow into that deep love we desire. I had to break open, heal, and then love myself. A part of my healing journey has been undoing the unconscious programming from my past and loving myself. Parts of me that were not healed became glaringly apparent after Todd's death.

And I'm taking Todd's advice to keep my heart open to whatever comes next. I have been seeing someone really special, someone so easy to love. Someone who makes me laugh like I haven't laughed in years and brings me so much joy; I know Todd led me to him. I'm excited about my future again. My heart is big, and there is more than enough room for all of the love in it. Every day is a day to cherish and live fully.

The other day, I drove by the site where Todd died. Everything was different. They've paved a new road there. The spot where his body once laid had a large puddle of water in it. Seeing that puddle in the place where his body landed helped me see that everything has changed. Driving by there doesn't sting anymore. Not like it used to.

Like the scene of the accident, everything in my life has changed. I am a different version of myself. I have not only survived but thrived—the way Todd wants me to. I'm not afraid to do things anymore. I cherish moments more often. I'm more present in my work and my play than ever before.

I'm doing new things I've always wanted to do and some things that have downright scared me, like starting a healing hypnosis business, writing this book, learning poker, going to the top of the Wilson building, dancing with strangers, trusting in love, and sharing my deepest feelings, taking courses, and traveling, to name a few. Life and love are not only hopeful but downright exciting!

Early on in my grief process, I was struggling. When I started writing this book, I looked around for something from Todd, maybe a letter I hadn't seen before, or a small memento, anything. I feverishly tore my bedroom closet apart, searching for something—out popped a little brown stuffed dog. Todd had gotten it for me on Valentine's Day years ago. It had a pink collar with a pink tag shaped like a bone, with the words "LOVE LETTER" on it. Todd had written on the paper tag, "I love you every day and in every way, OX, Todd."

"Every day and in every way" covers it all. It leaves nothing out. Todd was showing me that he's still here for me in every way possible. He will be here always. All of our beloveds are, even when we can't see or feel them in the earthly sense. There are ways to connect; so many ways. Many more I have yet to discover. The love never ends. It goes on and on, every day, in every way.

WISDOM FROM
THE OTHER SIDE

I've learned so much in the years since Todd passed. He continues to inspire me from the other side. I feel him nudging me to make the choices I want to make. He encourages me to say no to those things I don't want to do and make myself happy. He encourages me to live in the moment and not worry about things. Todd has inspired me to realize my dreams. He continues to inspire me from the other side. Following is some of the wisdom he's shared with me through Alexia.

LOVE & RELATIONSHIPS

It's simple. I'm not a very complicated person. But there are many complicated people, and they need to understand that no matter how complicated things are, there is always love. Even the simplest love can change your whole world for the good.

Brenda, I've thought about how we've been so meant for each other—soul mates—and we just know that no matter what happens in relationships and what anyone does, if you have that feeling and intuition, then don't let go of that. People doubt their feelings and they struggle with that, whether it's a boyfriend/girlfriend or someone they've been married to for 30 years.

You have to keep the faith. It's so important not to let go of that or lose it. It's important to help each other. Don't doubt your feelings of true connection. Don't doubt that person is your soul mate if that's how you feel. Because if you lose your faith, the rest will follow.

I'm so excited for you and the book. You're a traveling lady, always have been. I love seeing you go on your trips. I was with you on the last one to Arkansas, by your side. I like to learn too! So beautiful, this journey. You're a changed person. Even though you can't see me, we'll always have this connection. It will be cool to see how it grows. Don't ever forget the good times. The good times are every day because we're never really apart.

STRUGGLES

It's sad and tragic, but what we go through on our journeys is like a beautiful curse. Blessings in disguise. People die or lose things, war is waged, but it's all for a purpose. Let bad feelings or experiences go through you. Don't let them break you. It's the same for heartbreak or people getting divorced. You can continue to love that person and send them love. If you are not meant to be with that person, that makes you sad, but it doesn't mean you can't still have love and bless them.

Experiences can beat you down. Something happens to someone in your family, illness, death. Remember that feeling of love unconditional love and that will strengthen you always.

FAMILY

It is important to accept, forgive, and love unconditionally in order to maintain healthy relationships. I'm such a family guy. People today don't realize how important it is. We go through difficult things and still love each other. Family is the beginning and end of everything. They gave us life. I want people to understand how important it is to lean on each other.

Family needs to be more stable, with more emphasis on togetherness. We need to build each other up. Society is making everyone separate, and it's sad. We all go through so much in life. We can always turn to family. I wish I could have taught everyone better and at a younger age the way things were in my family. Lead by example, and your children will follow in your footsteps. I have proof of that when I look at our beautiful children.

Our family is our family for a reason. We may have had past lives together. We are placed in this life and this family for a purpose and to learn what we need to learn for our next lifetime or purpose.

LIFE LESSONS

The feelings we send out through our hearts are important. They can be curses or blessings. There is too much suffering. Think of the heart like a box of energy. If we hold in all the muck, we're gonna need some extra love. Let the good come and keep the feelings of love.

It's good to be motivated and have goals and things you want to accomplish, but you shouldn't be too hard on yourself or tear yourself down. When we're hard on ourselves, it makes everything harder. Depression, anxiety or other earthly emotions can block your flow of energy. Physical ailments grow from mental ailments and make things worse.

When people are on their paths and are ready for enlightenment, the universe will lead them to where they need to go. Call it destiny or fate; it's our purpose.

It's important to have faith in yourself! Don't doubt yourself. Your gut feeling is there for a reason, and it's something that most people don't know how to use. They don't trust it, and that is when they are led astray.

When you start to have doubts, do something such as meditation to clear and calm you. The calmer you are, the less worried you are, the clearer and the better you're going to feel about your decisions. People know that, it's just hard to do. Society clouds our judgment.

DYING

Don't fear death. Dying is rebirth. I have died in the eyes of everyone who's human. It's a big struggle for everyone. They're so fearful of death. They don't want to die. There is such an emphasis on death being really negative, and it's not.

It's truly amazing. We've both learned that the connections we have with everyone we love don't die. If we changed how we feel about death, it would change everything! Because death is rebirth, transition, learning time. We never stop growing. Our lives change others, and it's really beautiful.

All the experiences of our lives make us up as a whole. I did have a time of review. That's one way to say it so you understand. It's hard to describe, but it's really neat. You go through a biography of who you are as a soul collective. It's a bigger picture of who you are.

I know it's crazy and confusing. I know you're really interested in that, and I think I want to do that with you. There are some things I can wait to do because we are going to do them together. For some reason, that is how it is supposed to be. We'll learn together, honey. The love continues to grow even when we're gone. It doesn't stop. Our lives are like stages upon stages. Being a soul and coming to heaven is like all of our lives coming together.

ACKNOWLEDGMENTS

Dearest Todd: Words could never express enough my appreciation for you. Your beautiful love and support is never ending. You showed all of us how to truly live. I'm deeply appreciative of you, our life we built together, and I feel lucky and extremely grateful for it all. I am so blessed that you continue to guide me from your beautiful side of the universe.

Much love and appreciation for our beautiful daughter Alexia. Alexia, you've been with us every step of the way in the creation and completion of this book. You are full of love, creativity and strength. Yes, strength. We couldn't have done this without you, beautiful angel. So very proud of you and grateful for you. And to Troy, thank you for being a wonderful part of our family and taking good care of Alexia and Jackson. Love you. The world's biggest hug.

Much love and appreciation to our wonderful son, Dakota. Thank you for your help in keeping your mom grounded and being the "truth teller" you are(bear). Your humor lightens my soul. Thank you for being you.

Alexia and Dakota your belief and encouragement in me really got me through some tough times. And working on this book has been challenging at times. Thank you for your love and patience.

Your father is really proud of you both! And he wants to remind you to see all the beauty and joy in life.

Much love and appreciation for our sweet, smart and funny grandson Jackson (grasshopper). I hope you know how proud your grandpa is of you and that he will always be with you. Let your light shine!

Becky Costello: You are such a beautiful spirit and inspiration to everyone. Love you. You mean the world to me. You have led me on my spiritual path, right there gently guiding me to start a healing business. You opened my world in so many ways.

Jenny Canfield: You have been a healer and friend and your guidance has been instrumental throughout the completion of this book. Love you dearly.

Thank you so much to my editor Bridget Boland. I'm indebted to you. Your brilliance, patience and shaman ways are unmatched. You are a light of hope in this world.

Thank you so much to my publisher, Leann Garms and Abigail Dougan with BBL Publishing. And thank you to Jeniffer Thompson and Kat Endries at Monkey C Media. Kat, you talked me through some challenges in this process, and I really appreciate it.

Special thanks to my compassionate teacher and mentor Devin Hastings (and the three musketeers). Devin, you taught me hypnosis and that it's not our story, but our story about our story that matters. Hugs.

Much love and appreciation: My grandmother, Myra and my mom. Both of you and your love shaped me and made me believe in kindness. My grandpa Algot who taught me I am beautiful just the way I am. My dear sister Annette for her loving support. Your love has seen me through so much sis. Todd's sister Lynn's love and encouragement and our brother in law Tim for being the best uncle to Dakota. Todd's parents for raising such a beautiful amazing man. My big brother Adrian who helped me learn that people mean well, and we can overcome challenges. My little brother David for teaching me patience and the art of being silly. And my dear friend Joy for the many hugs, meaningful talks and helping me get through the most difficult time imaginable. Love.

Acknowledging my beautiful GIRLFRIENDS, pickleball friends and poker friends for keeping me sane, grounded and energized. I love you.

Much love and appreciation to Henry for your beautiful love and support for not only me but for Dakota, Alexia, Jackson and Stanley. Your caring ways are deeply felt. You've reminded me about true intentions and that all experiences lead us to where we are right now. Love you with my whole heart and appreciate you more than you will ever know.

Again, heartfelt appreciation to ALL of our loving family and friends. Much, much love! We are so blessed to have you near us wherever we may be!

From birth to death to birth, always by my side,
part of our soul family, togetherness our guide
Loving you comes easily; you see you are a part of me
My heart is open wide, forever like the sky

ABOUT THE AUTHOR

Growing up in Minnesota, Brenda Fletcher always knew she wanted to help people. So, after receiving her Bachelors in Psychology she began working as a Mental Health Practitioner and later, as both an Adult and Children's Mental Health Case Manager. But it wasn't until years of helping people in the field of Mental Health that her true calling was revealed.

In July of 2013, an unimaginable tragedy struck. After 30 years together, her beloved husband died suddenly in an accident.

Then, the truly unexpected happened. Brenda discovered love after life through her deep connection to her late husband. He encouraged her to follow her long-standing dream of helping people on a deeper level by becoming a hypnosis practitioner. It was through this experience of losing her husband that she came to know him and herself on a much higher level. She continues to communicate with her husband, seek his guidance, and feel the warmth of their loving bond.